The Heaven Treaders

This Is My Love Song

DAVID JOHN BURGIN

With contributions from Jayne Burgin

With love from
David and
Jayne

WESTBOW
P R E S S®
A DIVISION OF THOMAS NELSON
& ZONDERVAN

WestBow Press books may be ordered through booksellers or by contacting:

WestBow Press
A Division of Thomas Nelson & Zondervan
1663 Liberty Drive
Bloomington, IN 47403
www.westbowpress.com
1 (866) 928-1240

ISBN: 978-1-9736-0663-5 (sc)
ISBN: 978-1-9736-0665-9 (hc)
ISBN: 978-1-9736-0664-2 (e)

Library of Congress Control Number: 2017918294

Print information available on the last page.

WestBow Press rev. date: 12/11/2017

CONTENTS

To my lovely wife, Jayne,
Thank you for loving me so much. I so love you.
After the Song of Songs, it is our song.

David

For my beautiful David:

David was six feet three inches in height, but his stature in maturity as a man and in Christ was unmeasurable. He had the most attractive attribute I ever encountered in another human being – a clear and clean transparency of his heart. What you saw was what you got. That made him trustworthy.

You may think I am bound to say something of this sort about my husband and you are right.

After all, I am still in love with him.

FOREWORD

David Burgin, my friend, spiritual brother, lover, and husband spanning twenty-two years, has now gone to be with the Lord. He did not leave an inheritance of any value in the world's eyes. He does not have a gravestone for any of us to visit. He left something far greater. David left a legacy, a demonstration if you will, of unfailing love.

He left a legacy for me to share of his faithfulness and loyalty, his patience and kindness to others, along with his gentleness and goodness. He left a memory of his ability to overcome all things with an indefatigable joy and confidence in Jesus. He was never what I call a 'shouty' person. I cannot remember one time when he raised his voice to me or anyone else.

He was never sulky or moody. He did not need to be. David neither sought conflict nor backed away when it came to him. He sought to bring peace and was strong enough to stand in silence when any betrayer of peace should invade his territory.

David was not a member of any denominational church. He preferred to worship with a small number of disciples who simply wanted to develop their personal relationship with God and worship Jesus without agenda.

Most of all he loved and trusted God as his true spiritual Father with the dependence of a child happily sitting on his father's lap. He worshipped Jesus Christ as his Saviour, and Lord, and he daily sought the company of Holy Spirit.

David never kept a record of wrong in his heart against anyone. He was able to keep a pure heart no matter what life dealt him. He practised forgiving. This is how he was able to see Jesus. David was unafraid of any man and, as such, unafraid of unveiling the staggering beauty of his love for and intimacy with God Jesus.

He left behind the story of his own heart. I would like to share it with you.

What follows is a collection of our love letters, David's own journal entries, and diary notes of dreams, visions, and angelic visitations he experienced. The letters are written after the style of the Song of Solomon as this book has a special meaning for us both.

David's story covers a period of transition in his life when he was moving out of a place of brokenness and desolation, of profound heartfelt betrayal, through to a time of renewed hope, restoration, and peace with God.

It incorporates a selection of our early letters to one another, and as his relationship with Jesus grew, he recorded events that took place, such as seeing angels, having open visions, and hearing Jesus speak to him in a way neither of us had a paradigm for. David's story concludes with the completion of his relationship with Jesus.

May David's love story inspire, encourage, and strengthen

all seekers of love and peace everywhere. That you too
will know the peace that passes all understanding in all
situations in the loving heart of Jesus Christ of Nazareth.

> Blessed are the pure in heart: for they shall see
> God. (Matthew 5:8 KJV)

> The LORD knoweth the days of the upright: and
> their inheritance shall be forever. (Psalm 37:18 KJV)

ACKNOWLEDGEMENTS

Jayne, Joy, and Katie express our gratitude and thanks to our friends Paul Swift, Neil Grant, Joyce Lee, Jenny Quayle, Kath Tune, and Becky for their prayers and acting as a daily taxi service to the hospital and home again. For the prayers and cooked meals of friends who encouraged us to keep worshipping, for their loving-kindness and steadfast friendship to David and me and Joy and Katie then and now, with their persistence in prayer for all of us.

Most of all we thank our beautiful Lord Jesus Christ, who gave us such an amazing love story to share. For giving David a deposit of His love, that He would not let fall to the ground.

INTRODUCTION

David Burgin and his wife, Jayne, were a Christian couple living in a small town in North East Derbyshire in England. They were both married previously; David had two sons from his first marriage and two granddaughters from his eldest son. Jayne has two daughters, Joy and Katie, from her previous marriage.

Joy and Katie were David's stepdaughters. David and Jayne also owned a German shepherd dog named Jazz. They kept four free-range hens in their back garden and, later, three chocolate bantam hens. They lived in a three-bedroom semi-detached house decorated in a style they would describe as period eclectic with lots of imagination. This really meant David and Jayne were not hidebound to fashions and could always find room for any article they felt was in need of a welcoming home.

For a number of years, they managed an allotment. This is a piece of ground rented from the local council. It was approximately sixty feet by one hundred and twenty feet (imperial measurements), and they grew a variety of flowers, vegetables, herbs, and soft fruits for their home and table.

David and Jayne attended prayer meetings, joined in

Bible studies and loved worshipping God. They led small groups in teaching ministries and launched new outreach initiatives at local community events and fairs. For a period of time they used the hairdressing salon of a friend after working hours, to hold prayer meetings in the city centre. This was a particularly good venue because the salon had huge glass windows which opened onto the main street, and the public and passers-by were invited to pop in for prayer.

After twenty-two wonderful years together, David was diagnosed with terminal cancer.

The Bible tells us:

> While we look not at the things which are seen, but at the things which are not seen: for the things which are seen are temporal; but the things which are not seen are eternal. (2 Corinthians 4:18 KJV)

David and Jayne's story is about what happened when God started to reveal the unseen, particularly when Jesus turned up in David's hospital room and later as Jayne witnessed David's transition to heaven.

What happened changed their relationship with God forever and redefined their understanding of heaven and time.

Then Jayne began to piece together earlier experiences, prayers, prophecies, and promises. She discovered one way in which heaven broke through on earth for her and David and that the love of Jesus Christ is the same yesterday, today, and forever.

Joy Waters

You can have the most fantastic, romantic, amazing relationship with another human being. But even the best of these, where you believe God or fate has brought you together and has given you to one another, will end because all human relationships end. One of you has to go first. What do you do when you are the one left behind? How do you reconcile loss and grieving with trust and hope in a loving God in that place of devastation? It is only through intimacy with Jesus Christ as the only one who really understands what it is like to lose your beloved, and only He knows how to bring reconciliation. I discovered that God speaks to us all, all of the time. We know it is God's voice when it matches up with Holy Scripture. Not just the letter of the Law but the Spirit also.

I sometimes think it is funny that we understand international timetables for international time zones throughout the world and plan our movement between them accordingly. But very few of us take time to think about God's supernatural timetable and His heavenly time zones. God speaks to us from His time, which is out of time, but we often reformat His speaking to us to get His word to fit into our time. And that is when it is all too easy to lose sight of Him altogether. When we pause and ask Him to help us understand His time perspective, well, that is when our adventure really begins. We have all the time in and out of this world available to us.

Jayne Burgin

PART 1

-------◆◆◆◆◆◆-------

From the earliest days of our friendship throughout our marriage until he went home to heaven, David wrote a variety of letters and notes and drew small, humorous sketches for me that often included passages from the biblical Song of Songs (or Song of Solomon). He never waited for a special occasion or an anniversary but wrote to me whenever he wanted to express his love. I was never quite sure when he would hand me a letter or when I would find one in our letterbox. The letter that follows was a very early one. David did not date it.

The Lover: The Song of Songs is my song for you, Jayne; it holds my heart's desires for us – two hearts who have found rest and peace in one another in Jesus Christ, our Lord. I love the poetry of the original King James Version.

Behold, thou art fair, my love; behold, thou art fair;

Thou hast doves' eyes within thy locks: thy hair is as a flock of goats, that appear from mount Gilead.

Thy teeth are like a flock of sheep that are even shorn, which came up from the washing;

Whereof every one bear twins, and none is barren among them.

Thy lips are like a thread of scarlet, and thy speech is comely;

Thy temples are like a piece of a pomegranate within thy locks.

Thy neck is like the tower of David builded for an armoury, whereon there hang a thousand bucklers, all shields of mighty men.

Thy two breasts are like two young roes that are twins, which feed among the lilies.

Until the day break, and the shadows flee away, I will get me to the mountain of myrrh, and to the hill of frankincense.

Thou art all fair, my love; there is no spot in thee.

Come with me from Lebanon, my spouse, with me from Lebanon; look from the top of Amana, from the top of Shenir and Hermon, from the lions' dens, from the mountains of the leopards.

Thou hast ravished my heart, my sister, my spouse;

Thou hast ravished my heart with one of thine eyes, with one chain of thy neck.

How fair is thy love, my sister, my spouse! how much better is thy love than wine! and the smell of thine ointments than all spices!

Thy lips, O my Spouse, drop as the honeycomb: honey and milk are under thy tongue; and the smell of thy garments is like the smell of Lebanon.

A garden inclosed is my sister, my spouse; a spring shut up, a fountain sealed.

Thy plants are an orchard of pomegranates, with pleasant fruits; camphire, with spikenard,

Spikenard and saffron; calamus and cinnamon, with all trees of frankincense; myrrh and aloes, with all the chief spices:

A fountain of gardens, a well of living waters, and streams from Lebanon.

Awake, O north wind; and come, though south; blow upon my garden, that the spices thereof may flow out. Let my beloved come into his garden, and eat his pleasant fruits.

I am come into my garden, my sister, my spouse: I have gathered my myrrh with my spice; I have eaten my honeycomb with my honey; I have drunk my wine with my milk: eat, O friends; drink, yea, drink abundantly, O beloved. (Song of Solomon 4:1-5:1 KJV)

All my love,
David

The Song of Songs, or the Song of Solomon, was special for David and me, because it is a song written about two lovers. It describes the preciousness of their relationship to one another and invites you to know their world and how it is for them. It is about two people who are committed and devoted to each other. The events they experience as they grow together and a declaration that death itself cannot separate them. Their pledges of love and loyalty are completely exclusive to the other and utterly fast. The final proclamation sums up the beloved's ongoing desire to be with her beloved.

David and I were entranced by this couple's story and the beauty and wonderment of how this passage of scripture also describes Christ's relationship with his own bride, those who put Him above all other relationships and all things.

The Lover: My darling Jayne, we were destined to be with one another, written into each other's lives before we lived one day, recorded in the books of heaven. I am in your book, and you are in mine, woven and braided into each other's stories, each other's lives. God is breathtaking. I saw this in an open vision. I love you. David.

I have found all my favourite verses and written them out for you. They must be the Lord's favourites as well; there are so many about love.

> A new commandment I give unto you, That ye love one another; as I have loved you, that ye also love one another. (John 13:34 KJV)

> This is my commandment, That ye love one other, as I have loved you. (John 15:12 KJV)

> These things I command you, that ye love one another. (John 15:17 KJV)

> Be kindly affectioned one to another with brotherly love; in honour preferring one another. (Romans 12:10 KJV)

> Owe no man any thing, but to love one another: for he that loveth another hath fulfilled the law. (Romans 13:8 KJV)

> But as touching brotherly love ye need not that I write unto you: for ye yourselves are taught of God to love one another. (1 Thessalonians 4:9 KJV)

Seeing ye have purified your souls in obeying the truth through the Spirit unto unfeigned love of the brethren, see that ye love one another with a pure heart fervently. (1 Peter 1:22 KJV)

For this is the message that ye heard from the beginning, that we should love one another. (1 John 3:11 KJV)

And this is his commandment, That we should believe on the name of his Son Jesus Christ, and love one another, as he gave us commandment. (1 John 3:23 KJV)

This is our love story, Jayne, my beautiful wife. It is the story of God's love, His faithfulness, and the peace He shares with us.

David

When I read this for the first time, it felt as if I was standing underneath a waterfall of love just for me. I could stand, splash, dance, and sing in this fresh, clean, invigorating, crystal-clear water being poured over me through these words.

Sometimes we speak of being on the same "wavelength" as another person, and this is the best way of describing how I felt the moment I saw David. Even before we spoke, we felt it. When you have had this experience, it changes you both forever. It is the synchronization of a resonance of two spirits to the same frequency – we "clicked".

I am not sure it is even possible to describe this properly. I don't have the words in my vocabulary. I saw in David what he already was in heaven, and he was beautiful - no one else seemed to see that.

The Lover: My beloved, you have brought a peace and contentment to the most intimate reaches of my being; I light up inside as you settle the question of love in my soul. Your love is my Bethlehem-star home. We met and came together in God's house.

This is for you, Jayne, my beautiful wife. May this be a day of smiles and happiness all day long. We have been through some stuff, love, and we are still going strong. Praise the Lord. Thank you for loving me so much. I so love you.

This is a record of our journey – the letters we wrote to each other, the songs we sang to each other, the pictures we painted together, and the memories we made together. My heart has sealed them inside forever, home at last.

My beautiful Jayne, I am scribbling down thoughts as they are coming. My love for you is like the love between the lovers in the Song of Songs; they remind me of us. Our love has brought my heart to a peaceful place.

David

The Lover: You have unravelled parts of me I never knew. You touch my heart. When I first heard your laughter, I looked down from a balcony and saw your dark hair, your lovely face, so much warmth and love and smiles and joy. I saw such sparkling, shining, laughing eyes, and a smile that engaged with mine. At that moment, a love was born inside of me.

A peace entered my soul – a deposit inside I knew one day I would have love's permission to draw on, a love that I knew, even then, would patiently wait until the fruit in our garden was ready to harvest and then taste.

It was a feeling I had never felt before; it was a recognition of a shared knowing, an invisible union and a wholeness and unity coming together in one look, a soul connection. I never dreamed this could happen to me.

Your love and your friendship are beyond anything I could have hoped for. Thank you, Jesus.

David

It is difficult to describe how love enters your heart or when or where. One moment it is not there; the next, it is. You don't know where it comes from, and you don't know where it will lead you.

It is as invisible as the wind in the trees. You only see the leaves fluttering as it passes through. And when love comes, it remains and moves in your heart forever.

Jayne

The Beloved: My beautiful David, I am the rib removed from your side. And by His grace, God has brought us together and joined us together as one again. An indescribable peacefulness has come to me also. I cannot define it.

For us to meet now, at this time, is incredible. For two people who feel the same oneness in the same moment to meet here in this place and find each other such easy company is rest to my soul. It is so easy to engage with you. It is a sweet surrender to a beautiful peacefulness.

What a gift, to see one another as the Father sees us – transparent, nothing hidden, and no shadows in your eyes. There is only acceptance, agreement, and rest, drawn to one another. Come closer.

> As the apple tree among the trees of the wood, so is my beloved among the sons. I sat down under his shadow with great delight, and his fruit was sweet to my taste. (Song of Solomon 2:3 KJV)

Jayne

The Lover: Thank you, Lord, for loving me so much that You allowed me to meet my loving spiritual sister, Jayne, my friend, my beloved. Thank you, my beloved, that you have helped me meet my God and know His love for me.

My beloved, you are the only one for me. I want you. I need you. It is you and only you, my sister, my lover, my friend. I open my heart to you and offer from within what God has put inside of me – a deposit of His love, my devotion, and my desire to know you and to honour you.

Let the only debt I owe be to love you deeply from my heart. I have never known this feeling; you are so beautiful. I never want to lose this.

David

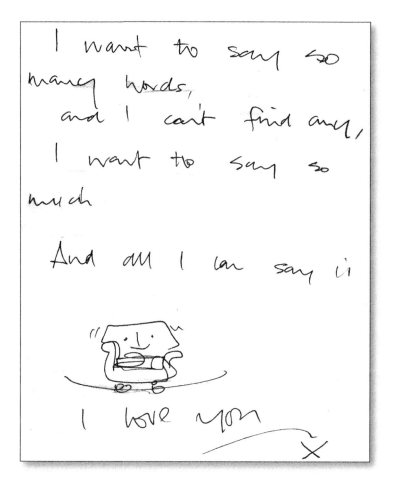

I want to say so many words.

You have found a place in my heart. Our love is as warm and comfortable in my soul as my favourite armchair that wraps itself around me beside a crackling fire when winter closes in.

David

The Beloved: I turn and look up, and there you are. You are standing alone on a balcony. I am stunned at your beauty, your wide smile, your clear eyes looking directly at me, as if into my soul, and I know I want to stay here, held by your gaze in this moment forever.

You walk slowly down the stairs, and my eyes follow you each step until you are by my side, smiling, saying hello. I am a visitor to this feeling – this unexpected joy springing up inside of me, being close to you. Standing next to you, I am listening to you talking quietly, our first conversation. My words begin pouring out, not knowing what I am saying, flustered, all my words spilling out at once, hoping you will not laugh at me.

I need not have worried. You speak, and your words calm my nervousness. You plant a kiss on my cheek, a softly landed token of your friendship.

You bring an unexpected feeling of peace, of tranquillity; there are no defences, there is no fear, and there is no tension. This phenomenon is a strange and lovely thing. You bring a completion, so quickly, immediately, almost imperceptibly, an unexpected dusting of sunshine.

You awaken my heart. You touch my soul. You bring this lovely love into my life. I have never felt it before. I hardly know how to describe it. It is a union between two souls, an engagement with an inner trust, and a completion in shared companionship.

I have no reference for what is happening to me. It is a gift offered and received. It is an invitation to know you, my brother, my lover, my friend. How did this happen?

With love,
Jayne

The Lover: There is a new excitement in me, Jayne, longing for your company, a yearning when we are apart, and a frustration in the time of waiting until we meet again. The waiting seems it will never end.

When I am with you, I want to catch and hold you close to me; I want to keep each whispered word. I search each meaning. I love sitting and talking and listening to you.

I hold on to the memory of your presence and the sureness and confidence of our friendship growing as I am getting to know you. Thank you for your letters and for your kindness of listening to me when no one else will. Thank you for not turning me away. I hope you like the daffodils.

All my love,
David

At this time, David lived in lodgings in a nearby village and in return for helping with the maintenance of the house and taking care of the large garden; his landlady permitted him to plant any flowers he chose and to cut them for the house and his own use. David regularly brought me small bouquets of flowers.

The Beloved: David, thank you that you trust me to hold the secret part of you – your own heart.

Thank you. It is a beautiful gift to be able to share your thoughts, your dreams, your hopes, and your visions. I love listening to you, to hear you speak of your hopes for your sons, of your aspirations for them, and of your own joys and some regrets. It is so peaceful to relax, listen, and rest with you.

There is a beautiful openness in your friendship that invites the same openness in me because there is nothing to fear, all things shared in this warm invisible room of completion that we have discovered in each other's company, a place we do not permit the world to intrude – where there are no interruptions and no disturbances, and where there is simply the beauty and preciousness of time undisturbed. There is the freedom to speak or be silent and know that peace is happy to find a resting place in both.

I love it when you tell me about the visions you have – visions of stars, new galaxies created, and prayers that appear as smudges of thoughts, half visions you do not understand.

I love the way you share your Jesus with me. I think this is the most precious part of you. I have never heard anyone talk about Him or describe Him as you do.

You talk about Jesus in the same way a relative would speak of a deeply loved member of their own family, as a father you honour, a friend you would fight for and a brother you would always defend. Your relationship with Him is so personal it's as though He is the one you have only ever trusted and every relationship is weighed alongside His.

You talk about things I do not understand. You talk of things you have seen in dreams – bright things – of angels and of a heaven full of light and colour. You try so hard to help me understand and to lift me with you to see what you see, taking me with you on a journey of wonder of love for God and His creation. I am so glad you chose to share these things with me. Thank you.

I see your spirit reaching for more – for more understanding of God, for more understanding of His word, and for more experience of the Holy Spirit – how you want more understanding of how your senses come alive in Him, more understanding of your own self. I see the ways you are always asking for more of His love. Don't stop. It is a beautiful thing.

All my love,
Jayne

Looking back, it is difficult to tell where David's love for Jesus ended and his love for me began. The line was always blurred. Most of the time it felt there was very little difference.

David prioritized God and his relationship with Jesus above all other relationships. I benefited from this prioritization, receiving the overspill of his love for the Lord, plus his love for me as his wife – I had a double portion.

It was David's relationship with Jesus that was the bedrock to our friendship, love, and eventual marriage. I often felt I was running to catch up with them both!

When we married, David continued putting Jesus first, and I learned to do the same. We grew in our faith together, reading the Bible, praying together, spending time with Jesus first, and then spending time with one another. This order was the most freeing, exhilarating, fulfilling, and rewarding experience imaginable.

Engaging with God through His word, engaging with God in shared worship with David was a holy place for me, one of peace and adventure at the same time – peace because all other aspects of life had to take their turn, and adventure because we could never anticipate what God was going to do next.

Our adventures took on many forms and expressions. Like everyone else we "did life", but we chose to "do life" together with Jesus.

We learned many things about the mystery of God's love for us by reading the Bible, studying the Word of God and praying. We both felt that as good as these things are for gaining a level of knowledge, there had to be more. Jesus had started us on a journey with himself, and he had no intention of leaving us at a level of knowing him simply by continually acquiring more information and committing it to memory.

Jesus intention was always for us to know him personally and intimately.

Jesus showed us it was possible to experience the love of Father God in Jesus Christ by the power of the Holy Spirit flowing without hesitation, interruption or inhibition through another human being to oneself. That it is possible to see the beauty of mankind in our redeemed state, as a new creation, immortal as we are in heaven. This experience of God's love is a living power that is continually changing us.

The Beloved: I have not known you for very long, but sometimes I see things in you that you do not seem to recognize in yourself. I watch when people dismiss you and ignore you as though you are not present. That is when I see your kindness, understanding, and patience and gentleness for people who do not seem to be aware they are treating you like that. Is that why you have not shared the things you talk of with me with anyone before? Is it because you know they do not recognize you?

I watch how you step over the offences they lay in your path and the humiliations for you to trip over, and I watch you refuse to engage with them. That is when I see the secret you. You never answer your betrayers. You seek nothing from those who attack you. You see provocation come towards you, and it has no power over you. I have never heard you say one bad word against anyone. Silence – how do you do that? I watch and see your kindness and your continuing trust towards the very ones who betray your friendship. Why? I have heard you say, "There are no bad thoughts in heaven." Is that what you practise here? Is this the answer?

Love Jayne

On many occasions through the years, David had dealt with all manner of challenges and confrontations for different reasons. Sometimes it was because of the position he took on scripture – it was the infallible Word of God and could not be compromised. Or it was a particular way he believed the Lord had asked him to conduct an evangelistic outreach event and others wanted to take control of it and change it. Once, he was publicly humiliated by a member of a congregation for wearing a butter-yellow bow tie, a French blue shirt, and red waistcoat in church, which was considered too flamboyant and irreverent. (I thought he looked amazing!) On another occasion he was told to put his hands down during worship because he was tall enough and "this congregation didn't do that". There were times when there seemed to be little let-up of this for David. The sharp remarks were as though there was always a small terrier dog biting his ankles.

The most painful time for David, though, was the betrayal he felt at the end of 1983 when he was told one night that he was not loved and his marriage was over. David had written down many of his heart cries to God. This was one of them. "It came as a hammer blow, I had no clue, but I can't do anything to harm my sons, what has happened to me is not to do with them." Sometime later he wrote with sadness about the manner in which his church had intervened in his personal life.

David lost everything, he recorded, "I no longer expect anything for myself" as he laid down his dreams at the foot of Jesus' cross. He continued to hope and pray his sons would pursue and fulfill their own dreams.

It seemed to me, reading David's recordings, that the

harder he was hit, the deeper the wounds, and the greater the betrayals only served to drive him further into pursuing the Lord Jesus Christ for himself. All that had been used with the intention of utterly destroying David had been used by God to complete the image of Jesus in him.

As I read David's notes, it reminded me of God's promise to his people in the Holy Bible.

> No weapon that is formed against thee shall prosper; and every tongue that shall rise against thee in judgement thou shalt condemn. This is the heritage of the servants of the Lord, and their righteousness is of me, saith the Lord. (Isaiah 54:17 KJV)

David dealt with all destructive situations the same way – he refused to engage. He withdrew himself from the situation and would not feed anyone's negativity or curiosity about him. When the conflict was immediate and the other person aggressively confrontational and David could not extricate himself quickly, he would let his attacker pour forth his or her stream of diatribe until the flow abated. Then he would turn and walk away in silence, never having uttered a word in response to their verbal abuse. He would neither attack the person or group in response, nor defend himself in any way.

During all the years I knew him, David did not once talk about another human being behind their back or criticize anyone regardless of what he was challenged with or the personal cost. David forgave everyone. I don't know how he did it.

Take us the foxes, the little foxes, that spoil the vines: for our vines have tender grapes.

My beloved is mine, and I am his: He feedeth among the lilies.

Until the day break, and the shadows flee away, turn, my beloved, and be thou like a roe or a young hart upon the mountains of Bether. (Song of Solomon 2:15-17 KJV)

The Beloved: I think you have an extraordinary trust in the Lord. Your trust in Him seems to transcend what happens to you, how others treat you. It is beyond my understanding.

Is it a mutual agreement between you two, Jesus and you? You seem so at peace with God. Where does it come from? Thank you for sharing it with me. I want to know that too. I am not like that at all.

You carry brokenness with gentleness, affliction with kindness. You carry sorrow and sadness with love and hope. You bear injustice with honour and courage, persecution with forgiveness. I have watched you enfold every attack with love.

All my love,
Jayne

The Beloved: I am so grateful to God that we met. Not looked for nor thought of by either of us at the time, we were each living our own lives. Then you smiled at me, spoke to me, and drew me to your side. I felt your eyes searching mine to see if what was in you was also in me. Recognition of something, an agreement in peace between your heart and another seemed to be what you were looking to find. The hope in my own heart is the same.

I knew this was an unusual meeting. We both did. We did not anticipate such an immediate friendship, a journey heralded by a new friendship that is full of quietness, stillness, with laughter and joy holding hands, two separate paths merging into one road.

All my love,

Jayne

The Lover Jayne, we have become travelling companions on a journey neither of us expected to make. I have no idea where it will lead us. You are free to stay or to leave. I hope you will stay.

Your David

David wrote this letter and gave it to me before we were married.

We had both come through a divorce, and even though we were sure of our feelings for one another, neither of us wanted the other to feel they were not free to end the relationship at any time if he or she so wished.

The Lover: Thank you, my beloved, for coming with me today, for sharing the joy of a simple walk in the country, a walk through winding country lanes little used by traffic, only sheep and soft brown-eyed cows walking slowly, swaying on their way to their milking parlour, tramping over Ramsley Moor and on through the ancient forest where silver birches are left to grow and then to fall, looking like sleeping giants covered over with deep, soft emerald-green mosses looking like winter quilts, here and there puddles of Kingcup lighting up the floor, to follow the course of the old riverbed, dried up now, with only a few twinkling streams left to indicate where once it flowed with vigour and power. We come across hidden ponds, glittering pools of reflected sunlight.

It is truly a gift to share a love of pond dipping, to look for water boatmen, dragonfly larva, minnows, sticklebacks, frogspawn, and tadpoles, both of us watching the honey bees as they land softly on the tall lemony iris. To share these few precious hours with someone who does not mind and laughs when our Wellington boots are stuck in mud, pulling off our socks as we try and escape, I love that you love ordinary things.

Your David

A stroll through a clearing of ancient silver birch

much warmth & love and
smiles, and silence and such
sparkling, shining, laughing
eyes.

Thankyou for sharing the
walk to the run — to see the
birds; the flowers by the
mill race; the ducks; the
fish breaking the water.

A walk in the country

I would like to take a moment to share something of the ordinariness of our lives and the similarities of our early years. We both came from traditional English working-class backgrounds used to having to find ways of stretching the family budget and making ends meet.

I was born and brought up in Northamptonshire and at the time had easy access to green fields to roam in.

David was born and brought up in South Yorkshire and had access to the Yorkshire moors and Derbyshire dales. We both loved broad open spaces.

My father worked on an allotment in his spare time. An allotment is a piece of ground owned by a local council and rented out to residents to grow vegetables. This is a part of our culture, and allotments for rent can be found all over England.

When I was about three years old, my father began taking me with him to our allotment. It made me feel very special. As I played at his side, I watched sometimes how he sectioned out a plot of ground for a particular vegetable, and I sometimes got to hold the measuring rod and string. He grew a wide variety of vegetables and soft fruits and used plants that complemented one another; for example, he planted marigold plants to protect tomatoes and broad beans from black aphids, and carnations between climbing beans. He said that as the carnations reached for the sun their stems grew longer and could then go in the tallest vases. My father did not use pesticides or insecticides and found that warm, soapy water was an effective deterrent to many pests. He used to leave a portion of the ground to lie fallow for one year following six years of intensive growing to enable it to fully restore the nutrients taken up by the plants.

I remember my mother purchasing large blocks of salt and carving it with a bread knife and crushing it with a wooden spoon, layering string beans in large glass jars to preserve them with about half an inch of crushed salt in between each layer.

The smell of apples wrapped in brown greaseproof paper always hung in the air of our outhouse where they were stored to ensure we had apples to eat through the winter months. By the time we ate them in December, January, February, they were yellow and wrinkly and shrivelled, with a unique taste.

Both my father and mother shared the work of growing and preserving enough food, making jams, pickles, sauces, and jellies to last until the next crop was ready to harvest.

Similarly, David's happiest childhood memories were as a small boy visiting his uncle Charlie. David was taken every Friday night until Sunday evening to his grandparents' home and to see Uncle Charlie, who was an avid gardener. David could not remember when or why or how this weekend arrangement started, but it continued throughout his childhood. Uncle Charlie had a very large garden plot on three sides of his house. On one side he built a greenhouse – sixty feet in length and about ten feet wide.

In the greenhouse he constructed a horizontal chimney on the ground, positioned along the whole length of one side of the building. He built a small firebox at one end, and the flu, when it was lit, carried the heat underneath a platform to germinate seedlings. Uncle Charlie grew all the vegetables for the family and took David under his wing, teaching him all he knew. David loved all aspects of gardening. Watching things grow, taking out the weeds, and transplanting seedlings into their permanent growing space and generally caring for the garden. He remembered the smell of the warm greenhouse, the smell of the tool shed, and the smell of vegetables pulled fresh from the earth. Most of all, he loved being able to join in.

Helping out, and learning every aspect of gardening, how to choose, grow, and then eat what he wanted, was nourishment to his soul as well as his body. The love of gardening never left him.

Many years later, when we decided to rent an allotment of our own, the passion for gardening that had been sown into David as a child reignited, and now I was keen to learn as well.

On looking over our letters, it is easy to see the early imprinting of our mutual love of nature permeating our writing, before and after we were married.

It is not surprising how this love of creation transferred itself to a mutual love of drawing, painting, photography, writing, and a desire to share our creativity with others.

It is also not surprising, therefore, that when we individually and separately discovered the Creator of all things, Jesus Christ, we would naturally want to share this discovery as well.

The Beloved: I love our allotment, the way you take time to help me understand and teach me how to grow vegetables and soft fruits and even trees, to plough the ground, prepare the soil, choose the seed, and then carefully show me how to nurture each little seedling and each tiny plantlet, how you watch over them at each stage with care.

You know what each seedling needs, and you carefully provide for each one individually, waiting for the first green tips to peep through the soil.

My darling David, I love you. I love our long walks, watching sunsets and sharing long slow evenings, most of all to know you feel the same, the feeling that everything is ok, safe at last, home at last.

You make no demands; you ask for nothing. There is no need for talk, only to enjoy the quiet contentment of each other's company.

To be with you, David, is the happiest place for me to be. Your words take a sounding of my heart and capture the echo of its agreement. There is an agreement of peace in our spirit, a comfort deep inside of the assurance of love's steadfast promise not to bring harm or hurt.

Happy to learn from one another, to grow together, and to discover one another's own pleasures and delights. You teach me so many things; you open up a world of nature's wonders to me, unlocking a door and leading me through a gateway into the wonderland of God's auspicious beauty. Wild purple orchids and delicate pale yellow cowslips cloak the hillsides, embracing the pure crystal waters where small waterside birds – wagtails, dippers, and moorhen – play. I think I should have known this by now, but somehow such an awakening passed me by until you arrived in my life and brought it with you. It is such fun to bake bread together, forage hedgerows, collect field mushrooms, and gather wild elderberries for a strong, deep, port-like wine, even to discover the simple pleasure of sharing a thick juicy steak on a white-hot barbecue with charcoaled jacket potatoes and roasted corncobs.

Ordinary things take on an extraordinary beauty. When we walk out together, I really believe we walk right through a secret doorway into heaven.

All my love,
Jayne

The Lover: You are my sister, my lover, and my dearest friend. Your love and your friendship will last with me forever, Jayne. Your love, my beloved, I will never turn away. This is something so special; I will not hurry our friendship or our love.

We will grow it together like a rare and beautiful flower and wait for the day when it is time for the release of its perfume, a fragrance so rare there will be no other fragrance to compare. This love is love worth the waiting.

I want to say so much more about what you mean to me – your letters, your songs, your smile, the poetry of you. How happy you are when you see me and when I come to you, you change my day.

I love the way you greet me, the way you hug me and hold me close for long, lingering moments, burying your head in my shoulder, touching my warm neck with your cold nose. Our kisses, our laughter, your easy acceptance of me, nothing guarded, these things speak more than I can express. What can I say, my sister, my bride? Ask of me and I will gladly give you all. My bones have found rest.

Your David

The Lover: Jayne, my love for you is a love that comes through Jesus, my Lord. I cried out to Him. I never thought this could happen to me. I never thought I could begin again. He has watched me all of my life. He knew all of it, and He answered me through your open heart, your friendship, my sister, your love, my sweetest love.

I will always seek to give you all I am, all I can, the best through my open heart. This is me, Jayne. As long as you need my love, you will have my love.

Our meeting is rare and very special. You have such an effect on me that I sometimes get my words mixed. I stumble and hesitate, but I would not change anything.

Being allowed by my God to get to know you is an adventure I never dared hope for, and I look forward to each new page, each new chapter.

Your brother, your lover, your friend,
David

You have woven and unravelled parts of me I never knew.

Your love means that to me.

David X.

My heart is unlocked.

The Lover: I am so happy that you can be yourself with me, Jayne; that makes me feel so glad. I love each moment I am with you, morning, noon, and night.

I want to draw you into my life completely, for you to see me as I am, for you to know me fully. I come and look for you daily, and if I cannot find you, my heart sinks.

Our language of love is our language. It is the peace we share, the memories we are making; each beautiful quiet treasured moment belongs to us, no one else. I could not ask for anything more.

I know your voice. I am aware of every tone, every rise and fall of every note, your laughter, your gladness, your stillness, and I want to come to you. I want to write to you, to put everything down about how I love you, a record of our love, with every detail carefully remembered, tucked away to be shared again between us in days to come. I love speaking tenderly with you, Jayne.

For me our oneness is like the oneness of my Lord bending down from heaven and grasping both of us into His own heart forever. It is as though God has visited us from heaven and has given us permission to be young again, pure loveliness, invited to walk in His garden with Him as our guide. He cradles us together in His protecting arms, and all longings eased.

He has invited us to share the secret dwelling place for lovers of His heart, hidden in His heart. This is where He meant us to be.

My darling Jayne, our love reaches its fullness in the presence of God. Somehow, this gift reached us from Him. We would not know where to begin if we were to try to find it for ourselves. These warm quiet evenings are so very special to me. I want to guard these hours. I will protect them and treasure them, your brother, your lover, and your friend, David. I have grown these sweet peas for you; they are an old English country garden variety and have a deep perfume.

Your David

The Lover: When I am with you, I draw you into the very depths of me. I drink deep draughts of love from your smile, your deep, dark eyes and your hair, the taste of your mouth, your lips, and your open arms waiting to hold me.

Resting, we sit side by side on the edge of a meadow of bright, golden butter flowers blazing towards the hot sun to climb and share the watching of a kestrel, gliding on the updraft.

I feel the softest touch of your hands stroking my hair, my forehead, tracing my eyes, my eyelashes, my cheeks, my nose, my lips. My fingertips follow the design of your face.

I cannot help but love you. My beloved, your beauty, our closeness, has captured me and holds me. It is beyond anything I expected. Your love and your friendship are beyond anything I could have hoped.

May you find my own soul to be a beautiful resting place waiting for you to share, to dwell in and to enjoy.

Your David

"But those who hope in the Lord will renew their strength. They will soar on wings like eagles." Isiah 40:31

To have sat and looked down on the wings of a kestrel, gliding effortlessly on the updraught _____

To have sat and shared it with you _____

I want to thank you that you accepted _____

You touch my heart;

Your love and your friendship are beyond anything I could ever have hoped for."

Simple joys

The Beloved: My darling David, no one has ever spoken to me the way you speak to me.

Forgive the times I am careless with your love. I never want to hurt you with my thoughtlessness or take what you have given me for granted. You are so kind to me. Your gentleness and your patience with me reassures me of your love. You know me.

David, you bring an indescribable peace to me whenever I am with you. This feeling quiets my soul. I cannot tell you how much you mean to me and that I know you will wait for me.

Thank you for allowing me into your world. You are a precious jewel, given to me to get to know.

I hold this jewel of you in my hand. I turn it this way and that, over and over, slowly, to discover every facet and then to hold it up to the sunlight and watch it shine and reflect a greater light, radiating like a rainbow of coloured gemstones.

Amber, amethyst and rubies, emeralds and sapphires, fire opal, aquamarine, and blood-red garnet, all cut with a brilliant diamond, every facet of you is desirable.

I love learning about you, watching you, listening to you. Thank you so much for granting me this beautiful gift. You make no demands, no threats, nor retributions. No questions, no empty promises, no guile or strings attached, you love me, as I have waited for love, without judgment or condemnation.

I love you. I have never known anyone like you before. I am so glad you chose me. I do not know how to describe how you make me feel. Perhaps there is not a word at all, just the knowing of you.

You ask for nothing, and for that you can share as much or as little of my life as you desire. You unlock a place in my heart I never knew existed. I was a stranger to this kind of love, the way you love me.

I find myself always looking for you to look at me. As I look for you, your form, your blue-black raven hair falling on your shoulders, I search for you and watch your eyes to see if they are searching for me.

I want to stand so very close to you. I want to walk in your shadow, to feel the touch of your hand brushing against mine. I wait to know the sweet fragrance of your kisses.

I delight myself in your company. I am not explaining this very well. It is as though God imprinted us, each with the other before we were. Thank you for the beautiful miniature roses. I am going to paint them. They are perfect.

All my love,
Jayne

This may be a good place for me to explain why I was so impacted by David's love for me and how it came to be that, following fourteen years of a previous marriage and two beautiful daughters, I was a stranger to the love David offered.

Following my divorce and still wondering what had gone wrong, I went for a walk one day along a quiet country lane where I knew there would be very little traffic, other than a tractor or two. I wanted solitude as I talked with Jesus about the years and events leading up to the divorce. I was trying to process the past, my current situation, and how I would raise my two girls without their father. I was now a single parent. I was relying on state welfare benefits and thinking about the sort of work I could obtain or the possibility of going back into education to work for a university degree for a new career, which so far had been a dream unfulfilled.

I was lost in these thoughts. As I continued walking I became aware of two dancing dragonflies in front of me, always staying about three feet ahead, but keeping in line with my path. I thought how stunning they were with their iridescent, transparent wings mirroring each other's movements in an aerial ballet, and I was temporarily distracted from the heaviness of my mood and unhappy memories.

The next thing was quite odd. I had a very strong impression in my mind of myself holding a newborn baby wrapped in a shawl. I could not see the baby's face. There was a light muslin cloth covering it. In the impression, I was trying to offer the baby a spoonful of food. I talked to it; I was excited about holding this gift of life from God. I was imagining the time the new baby would smile and laugh and talk. I felt the delight of an unknown future.

In the next instant I felt the Lord walking by my side. He paused in front of me, removed the muslin cloth from the baby's face, and I looked down, shocked. The baby was dead.

I heard an audible voice say, "This was your marriage; it was still born." I felt an excruciating pain in my chest, but it left almost as soon as it came and in its leaving left calm and a peace where the pain had been. The struggling to try and understand what had gone wrong and where I had failed in my marriage was no longer there. I did not need to analyse my past to find answers, because there were no answers in this world to find. Instead I could feel the love of Jesus as a tangible force inside of me. I knew He watched over all things. He knew about me and my ex-husband, and He felt all that I was feeling. Jesus had known all along the choices each of us would make in our lives and what the outcome of those choices would be. My first marriage was over.

Jesus was not judging or apportioning blame to either of us. He elevated the Father's love in my own heart beyond condemnation. I was free. It did not matter what others would say about me, to my face or behind my back, it would make no difference what my family thought or my in-laws. There was no longer any destructive power in gossip, reproofs, or cruel opinions brought against me. Neither, unbelievably, did I feel animosity to my ex-husband. All I felt was the presence of love that I could not have created.

This unexpected encounter with Jesus put something in place for me. I had often heard in church that Jesus has the heart of a lion, and I believed He did. But in this encounter,

I also learned he had the heart of a lamb, and He had shown it to me. I realized His lamb's heart was the tenderness and compassion that took Him to the cross, that He understood my brokenness and that I was not condemned.

When I met David, I instinctively knew he had also experienced a personal encounter with Jesus and knew the heart of the lamb in his own heart also. David would never hurt me.

apart. The sight of you
is something that
lights me up inside
no matter how low I
feel — and that I
can't do without.

My darling David, no one has ever spoken to me the way
you speak to me, I love your love notes.

"I think of you every moment we are apart …
Cannot do without."

Miniature roses

The Lover: My darling, my sister, I have been away from you for two weeks, so short a time, yet it feels like a lifetime of waiting to see you again.

I stand on the beach, looking around and watching the waves roll in from this vast ocean, and my thoughts turn to home.

These cottages are grouped together in a shallow depression off the road between Seahouses and Bamburgh in Northumberland. They face directly out to sea, and they are almost on the beach.

They stand firm and strong against all weather, giving all who are within their walls safety and warmth.

I have seen these buildings for many years but have not wanted to draw them until now. Now I have drawn them, I would like to paint them. They remind me of someone I love.

Jayne, this means so much more to me than I said in my first letter. I want to capture their quiet determination to protect those within their walls from all storms, lashing rain, violent winds, churning skies, and explosive seas.

I now look at everything with new eyes, hear with new ears, feel the power of God's hand in His creation, taste life as I have never tasted it before. I want to bring you here; I want to share it all with you, to walk along these beaches with you, to watch the skies change and the evening draw in.

I long to be back home with you. When I am home, I am safe again, with you safe in my arms and with me safe in your own. I am forever available for your loving embrace.

Surely, the peace we know, this resting of our hearts in the bosom of each other and in the bosom of the Father, is the same love as the love of Solomon for his Shulamite bride. I want to read the song to you over and over.

My beloved, I want to say so many words, and I cannot find any. I want to say so much, and all I can say is I love you, your brother, your lover your friend.

Your David

Did you get the flowers?

Cottages on the beach

"Cottages on Bamburgh Beach"

These cottages are grouped together in a shallow depression off the road between 'Seahouses' and 'Bamburgh' in Northumberland. They face directly out to sea and are almost on the beach.

They stand firm and strong against all weather, giving all who are within their walls safety and warmth.

I have seen these buildings for many years but have not wanted to draw them until now.

And now I have drawn them, I would like to paint them. They remind me of someone I love.

David Burgin x   August 1993

A letter

My God

Psalm 23

The Beloved: My beautiful David, I am waiting for you. I know you read my innermost thoughts. I wait for your kiss, your warm embrace, your happy smile, and your safe return.

I know when you are thinking of me. A bubbling excitement starts to rise within me, as though my spirit connects with yours, the anticipation of your arrival home. Though you are away from me, my heart is at peace, I know you are on your way back.

My eyes search the horizon for signs of your return. My ears become sensitive to the furthest sound. Thank you for the flowers, the letters, the messages; they sustain me. I adore the way you surprise me with joy. Your joy and your delight in me are intoxicating. I love you, David.

Waiting feeds our dreams, they will have their time my darling and await the perfect fulfilment of love's consummation. I trust you with everything.

Here at home, I think of the hours and the days we have shared and all the days we have to come. There is no need for anything more than to be with each other all my love.

Your darling,
Jayne

The Beloved: My sweetest love, your love falls into my cupped heart like the refreshing rain of a summer shower, each drop a separate, shining crystal of light, filling me, feeding me, seeping into my soul like the rain seeps into the ground, invisibly bringing life, sometimes a soft mist, sometimes powerfully, but always to be absorbed into the soil of my waiting soul, slowly swelling the seed of our love.

Your warm smile is the warm smile of the evening summer wrapping itself around two lovers.

Your tender careful attention is the attention of a master craftsman for his own unique creation.

I remember our first day together, your first invitation to share your day, and the day nature shared her delight with us in her exuberant vitality – the tortoiseshell butterflies, grasshoppers, a kestrel hovering above a rocky outcrop chattering brooks singing as they played over rocks and through whispering grass banks, cows with their newborn calves, a friendly dog, scarlet pimpernels, and damselflies glistening and dancing for our delight.

A squirrel feeling safe and hidden in the fallen trunk of a tree on the ground, warm, warm, sunshine, dappled shadows through a leafy canopy of tall trees, secret places, hidden places, we discovered and made our own.

I listen to you describe the beauty of a moss covered wall, the once glorious stature of an old barn, your favourite music, and following you into the inviting coolness of the shade of soft, falling boughs leaning to touch the ground with their protective arms, leading us through into a wonderland of awesome majesty, a covered cathedral of green. You fill my heart with music, walking with you, sitting with you, and feeling safe with you. Thank you for sharing the treasures of your heart and sharing your prayers.

This is such a precious gift; I want to learn about you, to love you, to delight you, to please you in response to your delight in me.

My beloved David, I love you, my darling, always.

Your beloved,

Jayne

Hidden in the safety of an old tree trunk

The Lover: Jayne, you are my lover, my sister, my friend, my bride. Who else could complete my heart's longing for such a love as this but you? One man made for one woman, each knowing he or she belongs to the other, a wonderful feeling.

A new world unfolded before us today, a world I have waited so long to see; revealed in this moment for us. The veil drawn back, the eyes of our heart opened, creation set free from her captivity.

To share this day and this moment with you means so much. To sit high up on a rocky outcrop and look down on the wings of a kestrel gliding effortlessly on the updraft is a simple memory for us to keep and to treasure.

To walk and walk side by side over moorland cloaked with purple heather, through ancient woodlands, paddle streams, and look up to a sky that looks more vibrant, more enchanting and inviting than a landscape oil painting by John Constable. From now on these will be our "Constable skies" – a heavenly canvas stretched out above us as far as our eyes can see – this is pure delight, complete joy.

The joy in my heart overflows as you take my hand and we rest underneath the canopy of a white-and-turquoise heaven above.

To sit and share these hours with you, thank you for accepting my invitation, my love, my friendship. You touch my heart.

I offer you my love and all that I am for as long as I can. I love you, Jayne. I give thanks to my God for the time He has given us to share. I pray our love will never be dulled or harmed in any way, and will always protect one another.

You give me so much, your smile when you see me, the sparkle in your dark eyes, the warmth of your touch, the smell of your hair, and holding hands as we walk, gazing in silence together at God's world.

Most of all, you see me as I am, and you love me. This is me. I love you, and I am in love with you. I am your brother, your lover, your friend.

All my love,
David

my love for you is real to me and like nothing else before.

These are thoughts and feelings that I've been running through my heart and mind since this morning. And this is how I honestly feel about you Jayne. I love you and I am in love with you.

This is me, just as I am

I love you David X.

This is me.

The Beloved: My dearest sweetest David, you knock on my door, and I open to you.

A map, a rucksack, a flask, and a bundle of sandwiches with a hand-raised game pie – a lover's banquet – what a spontaneous afternoon of glorious frivolity! How I love the things you do.

You are so much more than a brother, more than a friend, so much more than I ever thought I would know of you. What a wonderful delightful surprise.

You wait for my reply. Yet you already know what it will be, my happy companion. It is as though we have grown up in the same household like brother and sister. I grab my hat, and we are off.

We needed no words to pass between us. Here I am, always for you. You know where to find me. I love the things you do, the places you want to show me, the things you want me to know about you.

This is your radiance, and I am your audience. You have become a part of me.

> As the apple tree among the trees of the wood, so is my beloved among the sons. I sat down under his shadow with great delight, and his fruit was sweet to my taste.
> He brought me to the banqueting house, and his banner over me was love. (Song of Solomon 2:3-4 KJV)

You bring peacefulness like a calm, warm, soft dawn spreading itself over waiting water, stillness waiting for the sun's trailing fingers to caress the surface to bring the sleeping depths alive again.

We follow the river along its course and watch silver-brown fish move slowly, hiding and tucking themselves into the shadows of the overgrown banks, watching birds dipping and early morning mists lifting from the surface of the water as though breathing a lover's hush to move upon the ripples with an invisible hand. Thank you.

This is extraordinary joy, to follow the river until it reaches the estuary and the waiting sea, to notice the changes, moods, colours, atmospheres, the energy, and power, and see how the river gradually becomes less, less and less of the river, more and more of the sea. As we blend with less and less of our separateness until we become one, our love is like the destiny of streams to become rivers and for rivers to become oceans. The streams cannot help but seek out the river. The rivers cannot resist. They were designed to move, to flow, to be drawn into something bigger than their own selves.

We share a love of God neither of us understands, but we are so grateful to know and explore.

A strange and lovely thing is changing us. We do not need to understand it, only to celebrate it in joyful gratefulness to our God who knew before time He had arranged this time for us to find each other. Created before time began, our meeting place is earth, His beautiful planet, hanging like a royal diadem a shining sapphire of blue-and-silver wonder in space.

To discover His beautiful creation made for our delight, exploring and seeing His hand in everything. Thank you, my darling David, for this wonderful day. I fall asleep with the memory of you still beating inside of me. God has granted me the inexpressible gift of the beauty of you my darling. You give yourself freely and completely without asking for anything in return, and for that I gladly give you all.

Your Jayne

I enjoyed our walk in the moonlight.

I enjoy your company and your presence.

I love you very much and await our next walk on that beach

with love from your brother, lover and friend

David X

A walk on the beach

The Lover: Jayne, you have become a part of me, the fabric of me. You have given me so much.

Your smile when you see me is only for me. The sparkle in your dark eyes is only for me, the warmth of your touch, only for me, the smell of your dark hair, the fragrance of you I have come to know and to love.

I know all of you in all of my senses, and it is all for me. You stop my breath in wonder, the way you move closer when I rest my arm across your shoulder and then turn into me and let me hold you closer still.

I watch you without a word when we are out walking, gazing in silence at our God's beautiful world. You have given me joy through our painting and love in our writings. I love the garden we have made – a garden filled with birdsong, watching fledglings take their first flight; May blossom; fruit trees forming the promise of autumn harvests; blue bells: scarlet, pink, and silver-white rhododendron showing off their billowy blouses, snow-white daisies pushing up through the earth, shy forget-me-nots, inky blue flag iris shouldering fairy-capped aquilegia. Plump, blue grey pigeons queue for their turn in the birdbath. Doves wait, hiding their cream pink feathers and dusty blue collars in the darkening green of a laurel tree.

Old watering cans; brick-red clay flowerpots stacked and waiting to be filled with pink-candy-striped geraniums, trailing crimson nasturtiums, midnight-blue and white-star lobelia; an ivy-covered rooftop, home to blackbirds, a wren, a robin, and too many noisy sparrows to count; an old stone trough filled with pansies showing off their small orange-and-black monkey faces; a pond of gold, darting fish, water boatmen skating on the surface, transparent winged damselflies, spangles of coloured melody all around us; even the old wooden deckchairs with their worn candy-striped canvas seem to invite us to come aside and rest awhile, to sink into their loose-hanging hammocks.

Ordinary things touched by our Creator's extraordinary glory.

Your ever-loving,
David

Holding your hand when we walk,
Gazing in silence at God's world.

You've given me joy through painting
And love through your writings

It's just another part of you
that I love.

David X

Sharing God's world

The Lover: You thrilled me today with your excitement when I showed you my finished painting of *Rose Cottage*. All these things are parts of your world that I love and want to share with you for the rest of my life.

I thought of old Rose Cottage and the stories you share with me of your ancestors living there, a small, red brick built thatched cottage belonging to the church and rented for a peppercorn rent for the poor, of generations of your family living on the edge of the forest and on the edge of poverty, often on the edge of starvation, making a living as wood reevers (carpenters) and charcoal burners and of working the fields and picking hops in the season.

I remembered the photographs of your great-great-grandmother standing, smiling, leaning over the old wooden gate with a big, broad smile as though she did not have a care in the world and looking at the photo of great-great-granddad walking up the path edged with snowdrops, struggling with his old crooked walking stick and his old crooked bowlegs, of all the family coming together, and being told to stand for the camera for posterity. I think of their spirit, owning nothing of their own but love for one another.

In my mind's eye, I can see the rooms inside Rose Cottage – the big walk-in inglenook fireplace crackling with life, with its warming seats each side; the hot black range, its fire never allowed to go out; and even the hollow dugout of the stone floor and wooden beam above, cut and shaped to accommodate the grandfather clock because it was too tall for the beams of the low room.

I love listening and sharing old family stories, drinking a glass of homemade wine and journeying with you through your past where the rooms of a cottage take on a different meaning, where the size of each room is not measured in feet and inches but by its capacity to accommodate love, friendship, cherished moments, cope with life, and always have a heart that offers rest and repose for a stranger.

These are the unseen, uncelebrated ornaments of a truly wealthy home, a heavenly room, a place encompassing the fullness of the heart to overcome all adversity and to love one another above all else. I hope our home will always be like this. It is Psalm 23. You have opened your heart and invited me to step in. You have opened my heart and stepped inside of me.

I love you. My friendship, my love for you, is more than a passing phase, more than a distraction, more than I can ever express. You have meant more to me for longer than I have been aware, always there inside me somehow, waiting to be discovered, hidden, planted in a secret chamber in my heart, a room prepared by the Father, a gift waiting for me to find and release. Your love Jayne means so much to me.

Your love and your friendship are not something I could ever let go. You are for life. You are my life. You have become so dear and so special I cannot stop my love for you. I do not want to live on my own any longer. I do not want to be apart from you.

Thank you for wanting to share yourself with me. I so want to share myself with you, always to be a part of your world.

Your brother, your lover, your friend,
David

A watercolour of Rose Cottage for you

Poppies, Sweet peas, butterflies, bees, boats and sea gulls, hillsides, two people walking together and sharing a loving glance. Paintings and words of love that thrill and delight.

Thankyou for allowing me into your secret world of love, pleasure, silence, sounds and sights that excite and arouse my senses.

Thankyou for sharing your love with me. For caring so much as to give me yourself, your trust and your love.

I love you Jayne.

David
X

Will you marry me, Jayne?

Yes, I will.

On a warm afternoon at the end of summertime, we were walking over our favourite moorland. As we strolled along, holding hands, we talked about our lives, our children, and all the things we had shared. Taking in the stillness of our surroundings, we never wanted this afternoon to end.

So we decided it wouldn't.

Later I received this letter; it was a part of David's proposal.

The Lover: I have so many plans for us, Jayne; they are so near to starting, and yet I feel they are so far away. I love you, Jayne, and I want to be with you for the rest of my life. Our love has grown, blossomed, and has become ready to release its fragrance, pressed into the oil of joy.

I am your sweetheart, your bridegroom.

David

The Beloved: Your love has changed me, my quiet steadfast guardian, my protector, my defender. Nothing allowed between us, your love shelters us. You hold me and cover me. Your love is like nothing I have ever known – strong, gentle, protective, always concerned for me, always there for me, stilling my anxieties, quenching all fear.

My darling, we have been penniless, we have been without food, and we have gathered sticks from a woodland floor to keep warm. Nevertheless, we are rich beyond measure. I cannot think of one emotion we have not experienced together or one circumstance we have not endured together. I would not change a thing. Being with you is more precious than anything this world could offer. I hold in contempt anything this world would trade for our love.

Your own,
Jayne

The Lover: And when I come to make you mine, to take you for my eternal bride, it will not be with earthly things to seek your love with false design.

I bring a faithful heart and ask you, my beloved, "Will you be mine?"

I can only offer meadow flowers, a lighted lamp with perfumed oil to pass these twilight hours.

And when we find eternity, we will not seek rewards of gold, but only you and only me to be with and to hold.

I'll plait a crown of golden buttercups and rest them on your head. We will walk and talk and share all the things we've never said.

I'll thread a string of silver daisies, a necklace beyond compare, and we will be so close together love will fragrance all the air.

Thank you for waiting and saying yes.

When I speak words of love to you, they are from heaven. Wherever you are, they will reach you. You will hear them in your heart.

Your bridegroom,
David

When we were shopping and I kept catching sight of you, there was an explosion of joy inside of me — your eyes, lips, teeth, all shone with love at seeing me. And that is something I don't want to lose.

With all my love I love you Jayne — David X.

Walking down the aisle

The Beloved: My David, you continually introduce me to a world found only in dreams that passes through the mystery of prayer, filtered by my silent longing. You come to me and awaken my love.

You awaken me to a wonderful joy. My beautiful husband, you speak to me of love in every word, every gesture, every movement, and every thought you have for me.

Your tenderness, your sensitivity, your own vulnerability dissolves all my defences. You came into my life one day and in your coming brought a love from the realms of heaven.

You give yourself freely, wonderfully, generously, completely, nothing held back, protecting, caring, your only desire to give expression of your love to me. You step quietly into my heart, and I never want you to leave.

Your love is the richest gift I can ever hold, yet hold it so lightly. I cannot own this love. I cannot command this love and only receive your love as a gift.

All my love,

Jayne

The Beloved: I never want to be apart from you. Your radiance casts its glow over me. I gaze in wonder as you complete our bedchamber and prepare for the day of our wedding, painting wild flowers on the old, dark-oak wooden floorboards, scarlet poppies, purple-and-cream clovers, wild viola, tiny wild daffodils, lily of the valley, bluebells, and the pure white star of Bethlehem, with the slender rose bay willow herb and tiny, shy germander speedwell we met on our walks. I watch you work painstakingly on the form of each flower.

The delicate outline of their fragile petals is almost transparent as they provide a path for two lovers walking, holding hands, gathering items together over the past weeks and bringing them together in a compliment of soft light, fragile antique Honiton lace draped at the window to the floor and fresh flowers in a small crystal vase, our bridal bedchamber, my beautiful David, prepared by you for us, a carpet of coloured rose petals winding their way through corridors, up stairs, across a landing, creating a fragrant path for me to walk on.

I look into our room, and the perfume of deep-red velvet rose petals hangs in the air, a beautiful room, full of your beautiful gift to me, full of memories, full of summertime, of laughter, of playfulness, full of the bounty of you.

You planted a seed in my heart. You watered it with tenderness, and you protected it from thorns and cast away the stones.

You watch and wait. You keep away thieves and protect me from the destroyer of happiness. You breathe on me, and I come alive.

You cherish me, nourish me, and nurture my heart. I grow and you cover me. I am yours.

Your eyes watch me. Your face smiles in delight as I delight in you. Awaken me again, my beautiful husband. How do we describe or even understand what we have been given, to know that we were before time, and for now we are in time?

Your arrangement of our special place is our love on display, the resonance of our synchronicity made visible. How do we fathom our meeting in this world, should we try?

All my love,
Jayne

Roses for a Bridal Bedchamber

The Lover: Our bedchamber, my beloved, encompasses creation. There are no walls between us in love, not even the wall of time.

We are free to roam, to explore, to discover, to nurture and tend. Our home is all that God created for His lovers, His own design, for our delight. Let Him write His design in us, my beloved. This is our sanctuary of peace.

We have a peace that overcomes all obstacles, despises all offence, and prevails, peace filling our souls to the overflow, slaking our desert thirst.

Born from the trust of our hearts towards one another, we share the sovereign rule of tranquillity and harmony, a complete territory of soundness, abundance, fullness, and safety.

Jayne, my love, my bride, give me your hand. Let me draw you into our secret place where tenderness escorts us with gentleness and where our patient hope is not disappointed.

Peace has dove's eyes that rest upon the beloved in quietness and waiting. Our eyes find agreement in the other. Our eyes speak to one another in kindness, sharing delicacies from the banqueting table of the King.

A peace alights on our souls and breathes renewal into our hearts, bringing the restoration of dreams as it establishes love.

My beautiful bride, come and eat. Drink with me, for I desire only your company, only your companionship. Walk with me in the King's garden, where the Prince of Peace invites us, where the hosts of heaven worship all day and all night. What a sight.

Your David

My picture of Saturday is such a happy one because it's filled with thoughts, scents, sounds, sights and warm feelings of you.

Scarlet pimpernel, teasels, blackberries, Indian balsam, common toadflax, a dragonfly, a rabbit, butterflies, a welcome drink in a pub, a very special picnic lunch on a rock—№ 2,

to lay with you on the grass and watch you feed a pheasant from your hand.

I have no explanation for what is happening, I am just very, very thankful.

Thank you for all your paintings, your poems

Love is a shared adventure.

The Beloved: How have you caused me to know this? Do not answer. Let me press my fingertips to your lips; this mystery moves sublimely through my core, and I would not change a thing.

Our love continues to grow from the first hello, a tiny seed, a promise hidden inside. Like a fragile flower needing to erupt, it happened. Up through the ground, it grew invisibly – first a tip and now a leaf, next a stem, smooth as a willow, a bud, poised and waiting for the first dew to rest and sink like a kiss into the furled petals hidden within. Life absorbed into life's cradle waiting for the moment to come forth and reveal her royal beauty, a stunning mystery is unfolding, a word spoken and worlds are created.

All my love, my sweetheart,
Jayne

The Lover: To sow the seed, to watch and wait for the flower to grow and bestow a name upon her that only she and her lover know, and then to wait for the release of love's pleasing perfume, let the oil of each petal pressed be as the first pressing served to the King, my love.

I would wait a lifetime for this moment. I have waited for you, and I am not disappointed. Come, my beloved; wrap me around with the wrapping of your dark hair. I am entranced with your beauty; surround me with your loveliness.

You have put the sound of your love in me, a tune, a melody, a note, a music that travels from heaven itself through universes. I draw on your sound, utterly faithful, a singular dedication, the devotion of you to me.

My dove, our love is the sound of a beautiful symphony that has slowly gathered her orchestra and awaits the hand of the conductor to create the music that delights His own ear, our music, gliding through the night into the waiting dawn like a drifting serenade, poised, to begin the dance of creation.

Always your David

The Beloved: I love your letters to me. Please do not stop writing. The more you give, the more you express, the more I want to learn about you. The closer you invite me to come, the closer I want to be.

I love hearing about your childhood; about the hens your grandparents kept in the loft and having to turn the volume up of the old Bakelite radio so that it would be loud enough to mask the sound of their clucking when the rent man came; of the baby piglet you were given to hold on your lap on a chair in a room on your own, with only an old clock chiming its way every quarter, half an hour, striking through its melody of Westminster chimes; waiting alone while the hours ticked on, while the grownups talked softly in another room. You never did tell me why that was. Did you ever know? Funny stories of Uncle Charlie's home-built long, narrow greenhouse, with a brick tunnel running the full length, to carry the heat from a fire at one end, to keep the seedlings warm. A design he copied from a picture of an old Roman under floor heating system.

I love the stories of your ancient ancestors, hearing about General Gordon of Khartoum, a very distant relative, and the way your mum used to get annoyed thinking you should have inherited his sword. I am so glad you didn't.

I was amazed when you told me you were related to Florence Nightingale. You showed me your family tree and how Florence's family name was originally "Shore," her father being William Edward Shore, who assumed the name of "Nightingale" by the Sign Manual of the Prince Regent when William Shore succeeded in 1815 to the estate of his mother's uncle, Peter Nightingale of Lea. This having taken place three years before his marriage, it meant that by the time Florence was born in 1820, the family name had already been changed to Nightingale. How interesting, but what a lot of trouble they had to go to for an inheritance!

It is fascinating, though, that you are related to the Shores through your great-grandfather's marriage to Ellen Augusta Shore, the daughter of George Clarke Shore, George's second wife, his first wife, Ellen Lyle Shore being the line the Nightingale's follow. But how kind that George should give Ellen Lyle's writing slope to his second wife as a gift and that it eventually passed down the family until it came to you. It is nice to have family heirlooms and keepsakes.

Isn't it funny how colliding bloodlines change family histories and bring colour and romance into family trees? I loved it when you told me how you laughed to discover your ancestors were also nonconformists.

It was fun researching our family trees together and giving copies to our children. I wonder what they really thought.

I found it amazing we could trace your family roots back to the fifteenth century. Even more extraordinary, the earliest record is 1420, beginning in Dronfield, and you are still here.

I love our today. It is a precious gift given to us, to make our memories and chart our journey through time just as they did.

All my love,
Jayne

The Beloved: I love the way your eyes dance and sparkle when you look at me. I love the way your mouth turns up in a smile that breaks through into a wide, happy grin. Your happiness is infectious, creating happiness in me.

I love our today, when we travel at dawn and the world is covered with the gossamer shimmer of cobwebs spun across the fields like candy-floss silks, and we go to the place where kingfishers dart and flash in their striking iridescent cobalt-blue livery, where white hoar frost beads glisten and hang from every bough and branch as though decked early for Christmas with shining glass luminaries and silver tinsel.

My beloved David, you never fail to surprise me with your exuberant delight in God's world and wanting me to follow you at dawn into the unknown.

I love the way you search out new places for us to go and share a private showing of nature's amazing display, unmatched by any manufactured ornament, only we two here watching the dawn lift her eyelashes quietly over the world to witness the creation of a new day.

Thank you for inviting me to share your wonder of God, to share your private relationship with your Lord, to join with you and share your own private places where you meet with Him. Thank you for this precious gift. You withhold nothing.

My beautiful husband, my brother, my lover, my dearest friend, when the day is over and before we sleep, we snuggle up and go over every moment. These are special days, days to be remembered and recorded, days of warm thoughts, days of joyful wonder, days to savour, jewels bestowed upon us from His treasury, for no other reason or purpose than His delight to share His world with us.

We have set sail with Him, moving towards His place, nearer and nearer, closer and closer now, my beloved. One day, we will tie up on His shores, gathered into His bosom.

Jayne

Tying up on Father's shores

The Lover: Jayne, my beautiful bride, I have chosen you. The Lord chose us before time began. We are His plan – to find Him, worship Him, love Him, and tell people about Him.

Do you remember when I first told you I saw this? Do not worry; do not be afraid of anything. Trust Him. He thought of you and me before time began and then planted us in time, from beyond time. We will return to Him.

His house is a house of wholeness, tenderness, completeness, heaven, where patient hope has its reward, and He transports us into His presence to rest forever where He reaches for us and increases us and where our separation from Him ends.

His home is our home, the invisible made visible. There is so much more, but I do not know how to describe it or draw it. I have drawn a very crude image of us sitting inside the cloud of creation with God. We were there, with Him, before there was anything else made.

All my love eternally,
David

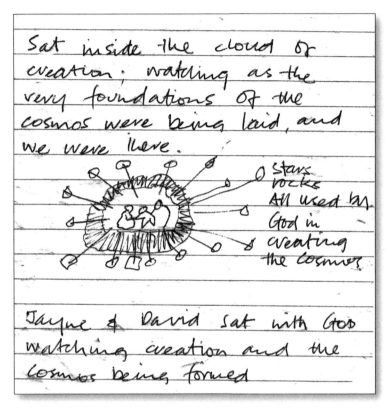

Sat inside the cloud of creation; watching as the very foundations of the cosmos were being laid, and we were there.

Stars rocks All used by God in creating the cosmos

Jayne & David sat with God watching creation and the cosmos being formed

Inside the cloud of creation

The Beloved: Therefore, come, my beautiful husband, David, with me through the veil, where love's eternal mystery cannot be halted or spoiled, where He takes us into Himself and our words of love become His words of love forming creation itself. These are the sweet pourings from His mouth of life, pouring over us. His song in us, creation has been waiting to hear, a part, a note of the one song that has been waiting to be sung before time began. Each note written on a scroll, kept in heaven, and is now unravelled for all to sing. My darling David, let the wind carry your voice of love and let the serenade begin.

You are my Solomon, my own beautiful, strong, tall, blue-black, raven-haired beauty in whom there is no flaw. We are His choice; you are my choice, my beautiful companion, I am your helpmeet.

All my love,
Jayne

The Lover: My dearest Jayne, you are my eternal companion, my bride. The fragrance of our garden is the fullness of God's world, with all manner of heady delights, where flowers release their fragrance for us all the day long.

Fresh freesias, sweet peas, lily of the valley, roses, lilacs, orange blossoms, all bloom at once, all seasons combining into a melody of wonder with butterflies, bees, boats on the lapping waters, sea gulls, hillsides, two people walking together holding hands, sharing a loving glance.

Paintings, words of love, that thrill and delight me, thank you my beloved for allowing me into your heart, your world of love, pleasure, silence, sounds, sights that awaken my senses from sleep. Thank you for sharing your love with me and allowing me to share my love, the love my God gave me to give, to express all I have held within me for so long and now at last, the time for happy release. Thank you for caring so much to give me all of you, your trust and your love. I love you, Jayne.

Whatever happens to me in the future will make no difference to what I share with you now. I will find you and I will sit with you, talk with you, paint with you, write with you, kiss you, be quiet and still with you, enjoy the warm coming together of our love for one another.

Our love contains a mystery we have never understood until now. It is the mystery of wholeness and completion in a union of peace. You are my sister, my lover, my friend, my bride. My love for you knows no bounds.

Your brother, your lover, your friend, your bridegroom,
and your husband,
David

I HOPE THROUGH THE REST OF MY
LIFE I WILL BE ABLE TO SAY THE
WORDS OF PAUL

" AND NOW I WILL SHOW YOU
THE MOST EXCELLENT WAY "
(1 CORINTHIANS 12 ᴣ 6)

BE YOURSELF BECAUSE THAT'S WHO
CHRIST CHOSE ___ YOU AND ONLY
YOU TO SPREAD HIS WORD &
INVITE PEOPLE INTO HIS KINGDOM

ONLY YOU CAN REACH OUT AND
TOUCH THE PEOPLE THAT CHRIST
WANTS YOU TO TOUCH.

" AND NOW THESE THREE REMAIN;
FAITH, HOPE AND LOVE. BUT THE
GREATEST OF THESE IS LOVE. "
(1 CORINTHIANS 13 v 13)

But covet earnestly the best gifts: and yet shew
I unto you a more excellent way. (1 Corinthians
12:31 KJV)

The Beloved: My love, tonight we walk in moonlight and watch each star appear in the heavens, like diamonds unwrapping themselves one by one, each displaying their own exquisite royal beauty, walking, slowly and quietly, beneath midnight's velvet robe, taking my hand, drawing me close as you place a silver bracelet on my arm, a bracelet of tiny silver-enamelled paint pans, each one filled with a colour from your paintbox, magenta, orange, and yellow, green, turquoise and indigo, violet, white and gold, and a signet ring, a seal of your love for me.

What a lovely surprise.

Your Jayne

David was a spontaneous gift-giver; it was a lovely part of his nature that there didn't need to be a reason or a particular anniversary for him to surprise me with joy. He didn't stick to the social rules of gift giving for special occasions or only on significant dates. His generosity was not hindered in that way.

David would collect wild grasses with a soft bird's feather and present it to me on a walk, or buy my favourite bottle of wine to share. Sometimes it was a surprise trip to the coast to eat fish and chips out of a newspaper wrapping, while sitting on the sand and watching the tide come in, wondering how long we dare stay, until our toes got wet. Or it may be my favourite perfume. One morning he went out early for a walk through the fields on his own to talk with God and came back with a paper bag containing three huge field mushrooms about eight inches in diameter. They were enormous. We cooked them for our breakfast with bacon – that was a delicious surprise! There were no rules. I still wear the bracelet – I am wearing it as I am writing, and smiling.

The Lover: The stillness of this night is like no other. Moonlight casts her silver tracings along this silent beach as we walk together, side by side. Only pools of reflected light where our feet have trod tell where we have been.

The waves lap gently drawing their own golden line on the sands. How can I ever explain how you make me feel? What you have placed in my hands, I can only marvel at. What you have shared with me, Jayne, I will always honour.

The most sacred parts of your spirit and soul, your thoughts, your dreams for us, your hopes for us and your fears, everything you ponder, and then you smile at me, as we walk through the night into the day.

My darling Jayne, this is so special. All I can say is, my bride, my beloved wife, and my eternal companion, how glad I am that we found each other.

There are no words to describe the softness of your touch, your gentlest words, and your loving embraces, smiles and silence holding the fragrance of you, the sight of you, the sound of you, the taste of you, your sparkling, shining eyes, deep pools of desire for me.

I know I repeat myself, but the feeling of peace and of rest, whether we are together or apart, is indescribable. You are always with me. Let me hear you say you love me again. I thank my God for this wonder.

I can hardly believe He has chosen me and you to know the eternal romance between the Bridegroom and His waiting bride. It is as though God Himself visited us from heaven and restored the years of our youth.

We are living our lives from two realms, a quiet stroll along the walkway where heaven and earth join. We have an invitation to walk in His garden, where all things are made new and all longings eased. We are His heaven treaders.

His love is cradling us, freely given, freely bestowed, and wonderfully delighted in. His love for us is beyond my comprehension, but this is who we are, his own children loved and protected by the love of such a beautiful Father.

As we watch the apricot sunrise on a new day, all things are lit up, invigorated with life again. We are alive more than we know. Our roof is a turquoise sky, our days filled with the same sweetness of love as when we first saw each other and it feels like a dream. The years have not let us down.

I play the journey we made to be together over in my mind. We made it, Jayne, love.

Each hour is a precious moment, each day a treasured picture, each shared meal a rich banquet. I love the ordinariness of our life, an evening stroll and a quiet walk, my arm around your shoulders, and your arm lightly resting on my waist, ordinary events that entrance us, daily happenings, things we have seen, watched, and enjoyed many times over, always new, holding their own natural unmatched beauty to thrill and delight us.

We hear geese calling across the heavens loudly, and we look up to see a skein high in the air, like strands of embroidery thread stretched out across the sky. Watching their arrow formations pass over our heads, we stare in delight catching this moment.

Months later, we stand, waiting on Hill Top, waiting to see the first black dots on the horizon heralding their return home, straining to hear their first throaty honking keeping the flock together, and we wonder how they make it back to England so effortlessly.

We are mesmerized by the murmuring starlings moving as one vast motion, dancing their own aerial ballet above the waiting branches, all of them wanting the same place as they fly lower and lower, getting ready to settle and roost for the night while the dozens of rooks in the village caw-cawing in the tops of the tall trees of the churchyard sound like noisy residents in tenement blocks taking too long to settle down while peace waits patiently to blanket the night.

You have no idea the pleasure I get when we go out walking and try to name every wild flower and grass we see, to hunt in botany books to find them. To come home and paint them together is simply glorious, to go out again and enjoy a picnic beneath a canopy of oaks, to visit the mill race at the old flour mill and watch, the ducks and ducklings, swans and cygnets, and the fish breaking the water. The hours we spend, trying to photograph the brown trout bobbing for bread and potato chips.

The spangles of sunlight on the water nearly blinds us as we follow the River Wye, winding through the old market town of Bakewell, munching homemade puddings and drinking hot, sweet tea from hot plastic cups.

My dear, dear sister, my lover, and my wife, we are walking in atmospheres of heaven to lay on a warm Northumbrian beach through the night, to watch the moon arc the sky and hear the ocean rising and falling, drawing deep breaths in and out, in and out quietly washing the sands clear for the morning, leaving jewels of tiny pink-and-white shells studding the golden floor for us to find.

Watching twinkling starlight and reflections of moonlight land on the glass bobbing floats of the fishing nets far out at sea, I look at you next to me, and peace is all I know. Peace surrounds us, protects us; it is our full provision.

Lying with you on the grass in a field, watching you feed a pheasant from your hand, relaxing with you in tired contentment. I will never take these pleasures for granted. His kindness to us is unexplainable. We do not deserve this intimacy. We cannot learn this, and we did not earn this. Jesus did all of this, Jayne.

I have no explanation for what is happening to us or to me. I am just very, very thankful to my Lord for letting us find one another.

I am certain friendships such as ours, our trust, our giving one to the other, can only happen once in a lifetime. I am so glad you have happened in mine. Thank you, Lord, for loving me so much you allowed me to meet such a beautiful, unique daughter of yours.

My sister, lover, wife and friend, it is beyond reason it is beyond explanation. I love you, Jayne. I love our love letters posted to each other. Don't stop writing.

Your ever-loving David,
Brother, lover, husband, friend

The Beloved: David, your love stuns me. I cannot find the words to say how much you mean to me. You are all things to me, all colours, all moods, all sounds, and all beauty, a rainbow released from heaven, lighted with colour and delight for me.

Red brings me the ruby blush of your lips, your soft plum red velvet jacket, soft to the touch; the deep blood-red rose petals kept pressed in a book, as a memory of our anniversary dinner; a winter evening spent before a warm and cosy slow-burning log fire with a glass of red wine in a cut-glass goblet catching the guttering candlelight, holding the flame in each prism until with each sip, the reflected fires slowly disappear as the glass empties.

Orange reminds me of the cool nights we sit on the edge of the crags, alone as the slow falling of the evening tangerine globe disappears behind the western hills and stoops beneath the horizon, bowing to the closing evening.

High breezes catch orange gold strips of cloud like ribbons trailing them across the turquoise sky, long, slow evenings, quiet and alone, no interruption, nothing to disturb our quietude.

We rise and walk through a Derbyshire village, where yellow-orange lights appear in old grit stone cottage windows. Curtains are drawn, a swift glimpse of a face and a nose peeps out as the bright orange of street lamps light up and glow without noise.

Shards of light flicker and dart across frosty, sequinned pavements, dancing and sparkling, catching each separate crystal playing with them, penetrating the pavements of diamond with spangles of silver and gold, red, blue, green, orange, mauve, each light a tiny star singing in harmony and secret delight as they land in silence.

Starting for home, the blood dark orange sun finally sinks into the night and heavenly stars begin to blink at us.

You place your arm around my shoulder, relaxed, secure. David, I love the comfortableness, the easiness of being with you. I love the way you make me feel so precious, so safe, and so loved.

Yellow is the bright cheerful sunshine of a glorious summer morning in June, jubilant laughter. You prepare a full English caravan breakfast to set us up for the day. Sizzling bacon, fat sausages, runny fried eggs, sweet vine tomatoes, field mushrooms, with doorstep thick slices of bread toasted on a wood fire that has drank all the butter spread on it before the plate gets to the table, mugs of strong black coffee and a map spread on the table, held down with jars of homemade fruit packed, strawberry jam and deep-cut Seville orange Scottish marmalade, while we plan a route, decide where to go, knowing full well, we will probably change our minds. We will not stay on the broader known way but search out the enticing narrow bridleways.

Summer beckons us to explore her celebration of life, joy without limit, playfulness, laughing, shouting, and running, leaping giddiness.

Yellow are the hot striped sands stretching before us with our footprints behind. We admire half-complete sandcastles left by other visitors and watch glistening gold-yellow reflections on the sea as the sun catches each curl of each wave and tosses it high, creating plumes of candle-white foam.

There is beautiful, beautiful tiredness as we fall down into the sand, exhausted from running and running, giggling with each other, laughing at each other, children without fear, giddy with rejoicing, feeling alive inside.

I loved the simple pleasure of building our own sandcastle and trying to fill the moat before the turning tide washes the whole thing away. We set off hunting for shells and hidden jewel treasures of the sand to decorate our sandy mansion.

You find a long seagull feather for a flag for the tower.

We watch our sand sculptures appear before us, as we dig and dig with our hands into the gritty beach and chase the sweet drip of strawberry ice cream as it runs down our chins.

Thank you, Lord, for this life, for the Father rejoicing in all He has created us to be. God is growing His love in us, growing His delight and growing His pleasure as we respond to Him. This is His beach, His garden, His Eden.

I love this place, gazing out over broad, empty beaches, reed beds, and sand dunes, green, rolling hills, wild green grasses with bobbing heads full of seed.

Drifting meadows wave their slender arms of green, beckoning us to walk through their fields full grown with soft, waving hair, the small, delicate straw of cotton grass, harebells dotted here and there with pure white daisies each pierced with a golden centre and one solitary scarlet poppy. What a vision.

Feeling the breeze on our faces, we watch it move invisibly through the field like a silent hand stroking each blade. Curlews are overhead, and we stand still listening to their haunting call.

Looking down, we discover all shades of rich, dark-green and russet grasses, creamy-coloured mosses. Small violas with their tiny, purple, upturned faces are shyly peeping through the shadows of the field floor.

Wild honeysuckle festoons itself along the tops of dry stone walls with flat, creeping, sage-green lichens. Curtains of striped ivy visible behind sentinel rose bay willow herb reach to feel the warm sun.

We look into the nooks and crannies to see tiny, tiny creatures going about their work, hidden. In the shorter grass, we hear a rasping sound; looking down a grasshopper is at our feet. It is completely still and then makes us jump as it jumps out of sight.

Walking on, we sit down to have a welcome cup of hot chocolate from a flask with crumbly, sweet shortbread biscuits.

I watch you lying on your back, looking up into the sky, not daring to look at me and telling me again how much you love me, wondering what I will say, what will I do?

My darling David, we live out of each other's hearts and minds. Never doubt my love for you, my sweetheart, my beautiful husband.

Arriving home late, tiredness is a sweet, happy tiredness of having our senses and our legs stretched. Placing a blanket at the side of our string hammock, you fetch our old, black wind-up gramophone record player and some of our old Bakelite records to enjoy an evening of nostalgic music.

Our picnic supper for two prepared, I set it out on the ground, spread on Aunty Nellie's yellow-and-white chequered tablecloth.

I hear you walking along the path, down the stone steps into our garden smiling as you approach. Carefully juggling a hot teapot and pink rosebud-patterned vintage teacups, a milk-and-cream jug on a brown-straw-woven tray – our own small English country garden.

I sit and gaze up into a china blue sky, Constable, white cotton clouds drift far above, and it feels like "on earth as it is in heaven". I think the kingdom of heaven multiplies when two people are in love, don't you? Peace is a living organism, a bright optimism that manifests wherever it is made welcome.

Blue cornflowers bob in the breeze amongst long-stemmed daisies with butter-yellow eyes, and you settle down with a paintbox, a water pot, and an old, chipped, stone, glazed marmalade jar filled with mousy brown brushes.

I watch as you stretch white paper and carefully prepare it to receive a memory. I plait small daisies in long chains wound round in a silver crown for your raven hair, as you choose cerulean blue to paint a picture of our day, trying to keep a daisy crown in place on your head with one hand and a paintbrush in the other. Then you kiss my cheek and wrap your atmosphere around an evening to treasure, to keep, as you record our day on a pure-white page with splashes of coloured water.

Indigo is a reflection of our deep intimacy, an intensive mystery; it holds in its secret heart all the promises of the wonders of love waiting to be discovered, to be explored and unwrapped and delighted in, shared passions, the fountain of life we draw from. Indigo invigorates us, feeds us with the awe and wonders of life. Royal purple is the colour of the King.

Violet brings peace and stillness. Violet is a soothing balm to our souls. Free of all antagonisms. My darling David, I love you so much. Sharing, joining, knowing, giving and growing together, reaching for heaven together, how awesome, we are crowned by love and gathered to Him.

All my love always, my beautiful David,
Jayne

The Lover: I love being married to you, Jayne; I love the way you write to me, the way we still surprise each other; anticipating the next post delivery with the anticipation of teenagers in love, never knowing when the other will write, always trusting we will.

You give me a strange, wonderful feeling. I am still special to you, and you are excited about me. You are enchanted with me, gazing at me, trying to catch a glimpse of me when we shop and end up in different aisles. I see you as I look across a room and see you trying to find me. Then you find me, standing before you, and a big grin spreads, and your eyes sparkle and shine with delight.

No part of you is too small for my keen attention. I know every detail of you. I recognize every note and detail of your voice, every move of your body, and every look in your deep, dark, shining eyes as they turn to hold my gaze.

You have opened the eyes of my heart. I have seen the face of love, and I am drenched with love's fragrance and perfume. This feeling is a deposit, a promise, the guarantee of love's eternal reward. I know I keep repeating myself, but love does that to me. I have waited so long to know this.

I keep trying to find new ways of expressing how I love you. What you share with me, what you give to me, is so very special. I want so much to be with you for all time, to give you whatever I can, whenever I can, and whatever you will accept from me. I know you as my sister, my lover, my friend, my bride, my wife.

I hope and pray to my God that we will keep on growing our love as we share our hearts, our painting, our songs, our lives, to build our home, pray to our God, and sometimes just to sit in silence and be with Him together.

How relaxing it is to be in company where we do not have to ask permissions from the other or apologize for imagined offences, what peace. I am me, Jayne, and this is my love for you. I have waited for this all of my life; I have never known this until now.

The years we have been married have not diminished our love; it has not decreased but increased in all the things life has delivered to us to navigate our way through together. Love causes us to grow into God together.

We grow together deeper and deeper. I will always be your brother, your lover, your friend, your bridegroom, your faithful husband, your loyal companion.

Your love and your friendship, your eternal companionship, is beyond anything I could ever have hoped.

In the beginning God created the heaven and the earth (Genesis 1:1 KJV) and *you* and *me*!

David

The Beloved: My beautiful one, David, your love and your friendship are beyond anything I could ever have hoped. My beloved husband, I cannot express my utter delight in the way you cause me to release myself to you.

Sometimes quietly, sometimes noisily, sometimes powerfully, sometimes softly, sometimes passionately, and always fully, instinctively I offer myself to you. You lift my spirit; you tenderly hold my heart in your hands in exchange for your own. Thank you for faithfully releasing the song of intimacy in your heart. Your staggering beauty captivates me in wonder and joy. Your unveiled glory set aside only for me.

Surrender is intoxicating.

Jayne

The Lover: Jayne, my love for you continues to deepen over time. It is a love I always hoped for, always believed existed somewhere but almost gave up thinking I would ever know. I never really dreamed or hoped or dared imagine this would have happened to me. It was always something I thought other couples experienced.

I feel that I have known you for a very long time, longer than it is. There is timelessness about our love, and I love all of it. I want to shout from the rooftops, "I love you Jayne."

You touch my heart in a way I cannot explain. I am so happy that you continue to share yourself with me freely, that you trust me; you have complete confidence in my love for you. Sitting holding you, kissing you, I am young again, with the first rush of surprise at love's arrival.

I enjoy the way we are with each other. I enjoy our laughter. I want to be around you always, Jayne, to share our lives forever. Walking, talking, painting, writing, singing, building, gardening, working, loving, we are two people that have become one, rejoicing in what our God has given us.

I hope I don't go on too much, but you are the only person who has ever laughed with me and cried with me. You are the only one who has ever wept for me and told me you could not live without me, that you don't want to lose me. Jayne, you are the only one.

Even when we are doing chores, I look at you, and the sight of you triggers an explosion of joy inside me. Deep, dark-brown, sparkling eyes, your lips, your teeth, your smile, your form, all shine with loving me, and I need to drink and drink and drink.

Our love is something I could never have imagined

could be real, getting to know each other's ways, characters, personalities, hopes, dreams, and the joy and pleasure of exploring and knowing each other's hearts moment by moment by moment. To see your spirit, to know your soul, I could never have dreamed God could have this for me, yet it is all true.

I have no explanations, Jayne. All I know is that I love you and will continue to give you all I can. I smile inside because of you. I am part of your life, this year, next year, every year, the next, the next, the next.

This is how you make me feel, your love and friendship mean oh so much to me. You make me reach higher and higher.

The Beloved: All the beautiful things of you, my darling David, all that we feel, all we write to each other is a beautiful journey, a journey we never expected to be taking together. I am so glad we are. I feel the same as you, my darling. It is the most amazing gift, to meet someone who enjoys so many of the same simple pastimes.

Simple pleasures that bring us so much fun and laughter, and so much gentle loving – building a greenhouse together, building a tomato house, planting fruit trees and soft fruit plants, pickling onions and making jam, choosing our hens and laughing when the girls told us what they had named them: Hippolyta, Titania, Aleta and Dorita, Caramacky, and Cheeky Hen (also known as Baby Hen, Chicken Pie, Chick Pea, or anything else we think of impulsively), trying to find them in the dark at night to put them into their shed, panicking because we could not find them at first, and discovering they had roosted on the windowsills of the house.

Every time we try something new, it is as though God is encouraging us Himself, saying, "Have a go," "Try this," "This is fun," "See what happens," "Be fearless." He takes us by the hand and by surprise. I do not know how else to describe the joy of each new thing He shows us.

We have no idea where we are going with Him or what we will do, or really, what the plan is.

What is the plan? It is an amazing adventure.

I love you, my darling. You have brought miracles into my life. You have brought the fulfilment of my dreams; I want to be a part of yours.

You have brought so much to me. You have expanded my dreams until our horizons have no boundaries. Your love is without condition or expectation of perfection or performance. Your patience is kindness to the marrow of my bones. Your smile says, "I see beyond what others see. I see beyond what you see in yourself. I see you, made in the image of God." You love me with all of my character flaws. You pick me up when I fall and heal the battering and pummelling of life.

All my love,
Your Jayne

The Beloved: If I were to spend one night without you, I would be lost. Your love shapes my life and all of my desires.

You have built a home for us where peace prevails. You laid a new floor, rebuilt the walls, built our red brick fireplace, and fetched an oak-log gatepost for a mantel. I watch you taking hours carving and smoothing and polishing roots of trees to make ornaments for our home. You have created a home where God is always welcome and where your spirit calls me in the night, drawing me to your side, where the poetry of your soul consumes me.

You have created the home of our dreams for us, a home that says come in, sit down, put your feet up, and breathe. These are the unseen, uncelebrated ornaments of a truly wealthy home, a heavenly room, a place encompassing the fullness of the heart. Our home will always be like this, because you have made it so.

My beautiful David, your love is the first sound I hear, the first songbird of spring, the first warm days of summer's china-blue skies, the promised richness of autumn's orange gold with the quiet tranquillity of hidden things growing under the protection of winter snows.

For me to stand next to a man like you, I can only wonder at and receive as a gift of God. He brought you into my life, and you taught me to know who I am. I read our letters, our songs repeatedly, remembering all the things we have gone through, all our first beginnings, our confessions to one another, our longing for one another and the slow persevering path we trod to be with one another. Wherever that path continues takes us, we go together. We go higher.

David, I love you more now than when my eyes first saw

you, more now as each year brings a new expression of our love and a new adventure, the promised maturing of His heart in us.

I sometimes wonder if we decide to do things or the Lord has prepared things in advance for us to do. He says He has. I can hardly believe it is possible outside of heaven itself, but it is all true because we are living it.

He has entrusted us with a precious gift. He has invited us to be a part of His own glorious romance with humankind.

If I give you all I am, it can never be enough; you are my song of songs, my utter delight, my King Solomon, my beautiful, tall, raven-haired beauty.

Your Jayne

David, my husband,

Make haste, my beloved, and be thou like to a roe or to a young hart upon the mountains of spices.
(Song of Solomon 8:14 KJV)

Mountains of spices

The Lover: It seems you have always been a part of my life. For as long as I have known you, I have been in love with you from the very first time, I saw you from a balcony and later as I stood listening to you rehearsing with a choir and watched you rehearse with a drama group for a production of the fairy tale "Puss in Boots", with a hundred other moments reinforcing the other, affirming and confirming I needed to get to know you.

For me, just to see you is so warming and so special. I cannot express any other way than to say I fell in love with you all those years ago. My love for you is still real and like nothing else before.

These are thoughts and feelings that I have been running through my heart and mind since this morning. This is how I honestly feel about you all of the time, since I first saw you. Jayne, I loved you, and I am in love with you. This is me; still, just as I am I love you.

Meeting you changed everything.

Sharing our Saturday walk in the countryside is such a happy one, filled with memories of enjoying simple pleasures, caught and held forever, exploring an herb garden, wandering around old fish ponds once used to feed quarrymen in the grit-stone dales, collecting fir cones, finding the glass-blower's house and buying "the earth" captured in a transparent glass ball, discovering the rocking horse carver in his workshop and watching him lovingly comb out the white mane and tail of his latest steed, scents, sounds and sights all colours, expressions and experiences of our love.

We found purple and yellow violas hidden in a meadow,

speedwell and teasels, blackberries, Indian balsam, common toadflax, shimmering dragonfly and demoiselles, and a tiny rabbit nibbling a hasty meal, butterflies, a welcome drink in a friendly pub. We shared a very special picnic lunch on a rock for two.

I love the way you smiled and laughed with such open pleasure at the bouquet I made for you – crimson clovers with heads like bursting pomegranates, wild daisies, rich buttery buttercups, dandelions with their golden fronds as long as a lion's mane, a wild rose, with the shy blue and pink forget-me-not, all tied up with a sash of glossy green ivy.

We stayed and looked at the seeds of an alder tree to see how God had made them. We found nuts nibbled by squirrels, and we found a secret place, a grove where dappled sunshine broke through the cathedral canopy above, and we lay down to watch the shafts of golden light fall silently through the branches to the ground. The earth was warm, the only sound the small birds and distant laughter of children on the boating lake.

The sun wrapped its warm and loving arms around us, as you did to me. You have given me so much; you will always have me, Jayne.

Your ever-loving husband,
David

July 03

I'd like to weave you memories,
I'd like to spin you dreams,
with words to paint a tapestry
of all life's hopes and schemes.
Sweet songs of love I'd like to sing
your senses to beguile.
But most of all I'd like to bring
you laughter for a while.

For dreams are passing things I fear
hope is often all too fleeting.
So many loves end with a tear
despite fond heart's entreating.
And memories gain their rosy hue
when reality's long gone.
So smiles are what I'd bring to you
and laughter from now on.

Sweet songs of love

The Beloved: I can feel all that is going on inside of you. I cannot help it. I hear your voice singing softly to me when you think I am asleep. I know you are watching me, and your sound draws me, travelling through my soul resonating in perfect balance. You are unafraid of what the future holds; you are strong for me. I see your invisible stature, I see your radiance, I see your beauty, and I lose myself in the wonder of you. This extraordinary peace quells all the siren songs of the world. Their siren voices do not have the power to disturb me.

You hold me without condition or reservation. You continually astound me. We are in Eden again, where Jesus has brought us into His garden to eat from the tree of life. His heart is altogether lovely. God is the source of all love, and He has deposited a piece of His love in us to do with whatever we would choose. He trusts us. He opened a doorway, and we dared step through to enjoy His company, because He enjoys ours. Isn't that amazing love?

All my love, darling,
Jayne

The Lover: Lord, thank you, for allowing me to meet such a unique and beautiful daughter of yours. Thank you for bringing me someone I find so easy to love, who asks for nothing, who puts no pressure on me for anything, and therefore, I give all I can.

I hope through the rest of my life I will be able to say the words of Paul the Apostle:

> But covet earnestly the best gifts: and yet shew I unto you a more excellent way. (1 Corinthians 12:31 KJV)

> Though I speak with the tongues of men and of angels, and have not charity, I am become as sounding brass, or a tinkling cymbal.
> And though I have the gift of prophecy, and understand all mysteries, and all knowledge; and though I have all faith, so that I could remove mountains, and have not charity, I am nothing.
> And though I bestow all my goods to feed the poor, and though I give my body to be burned, and have not charity, It profiteth me nothing.
> Charity suffereth long, and is kind; charity envieth not; charity vaunteth not itself, is not puffed up,
> Doth not behave itself unseemly, seeketh not her own, is not easily provoked, thinketh no evil;
> Rejoiceth not in iniquity, but rejoiceth in the truth;
> Beareth all things, believeth all things, hopeth all things, endureth all things.
> Charity never faileth: but whether there be prophecies, they shall fail; whether there

be tongues, they shall cease; whether there be knowledge, it shall vanish away.

For we know in part, and we prophecy in part.

But when that which is perfect is come, then that which is in part shall be done away.

When I was a child, I spake as a child, I understood as a child, I thought as a child: but when I became a man, I put away childish things.

For now we see through a glass, darkly; but then face to face: now I know in part; but then shall I know even as also I am known.

And now abideth faith, hope, charity, these three; but the greatest of these is charity. (1 Corinthians 13:1-13 KJV)

The Beloved: Our peace is complete when we are alone together. We look for no other place to be, no other one to be with, beyond the reach of time. Thank you for teaching me to hear your voice in silence, for allowing me to follow you behind the veil, to draw the curtain and see what you see. Help me learn more of this beautiful place where quietness is content to trace the mystery of you without words.

You invite me into this private world, this territory of your soul with hidden places where only love's footprint is permitted to linger, without walls, no part of you withheld, no walled off places in your heart. Lead me again into new and lovely lands, places I've never seen, worlds I could never have imagined existed.

This landscape of you is more beautiful than anything this world can offer, new unexplored territory; this place where there is more sunshine, more light, more radiance, more joy, more giving, more receiving, more colour, more feeling, more life, and, oh, so much more love. There is a glory hidden here not seen by the world, where everything of the world is outside. How do I describe this place? What colours would I use? A paintbox does not hold enough.

I bring you the first blush of a rose, the purity of the first snowfall, the twilight hush of the first evening, and trace the pattern of the first demoiselle's wings. I bring you our first smile, our first walk. I summon from the ends of the earth the fragrance of our first summer.

I bring you the first stars as we sit beneath their first light. I bring all our first thoughts of love, captured in the first moment of time. Threading the first morning's cobwebs on a spool for you as they spin the fields with silver candy floss, we unravel the mystery of the first dew on the first grass as we sit on quilted cushions of velvet moss.

Jayne

The Lover and His Beloved; Gathered into the atmosphere of eternal protection, to drink from the well that never runs dry, always flowing, always refreshing, always there, Quenching our thirst for life, drenching us with a sense of indescribable completeness, the place we have been searching to find is here.

We have found the culmination. Goal of our journey, our waiting over. An audience with Him is the presence of pure goodness, pure worship, pure glory. He reaches out to us, enveloping us, and our separateness is lost in His embrace forever.

The presence of love, how do we describe His fearful awesomeness – a fearfulness that compels us to kneel before Him at the same time as flooding us with His compassionate love that bids us to stand and invites us to look into His face so that we will see for ourselves how much He loves us and does not condemn us?

What do we see in His eyes as they penetrate us? In His eyes, we see love for us there are no words to describe. To call Him love is not love enough. To call Him mercy is not mercy enough. To name Him fear is not the right fear. He is simply All Mighty. Even that is too simple. To call Him faithful does not do justice to His faithfulness. To call Him Lord, to call Him Father, to call Him friend, these names we name Him with, He loves, but even these cannot describe who He is. He created us to find Him. However, we did not find Him, but He found us on our wanderings. He chose to walk alongside us on our path and to reveal Himself to us.

We walk with Him, we talk with Him, and we journey over hills, beside rivers, through woodland groves, and look down from mountaintops with Him. We walk through fire, but it only refines us as we dance in the flames together. We hang on every word He whispers, we notice every gesture He makes, and we cannot thank Him enough.

We rest for a while and sit listening to the silence. We sit with our knees tucked under our chins, watching and waiting for the mystery of the birth of creation to begin.

A sunbeam flashes, it rolls, and it splashes, and a rainbow is born. Your hand reaches mine, and we walk for a while at the end of the day. We hear a new sound, His voice getting closer, calling, "Lovers, come away." He reaches for us, teaches us, to go further and deeper, higher than we have been before.

I see sand like a shimmering golden dune between heaven and earth. A trickle is falling, gaining momentum until it becomes a landslide with more and more streams running together, each tiny particle each grain rolling against another. Each grain is moving, brushing, and nudging, sweeping, sliding, spinning, singing its way to the earth like a mountain of moving, dancing particles of golden sunlight, turning around, looking this way and that, unstoppable. Each outline becoming distinct as it nears the ground and becomes visible. The angels are coming, and some are here already to herald His return.

This is the season we get to see the immortal ones.

The Lover: My whole life is changed by love. I am made new by God's love for us, by our love for Him. I have hopes and dreams for us, my darling Jayne, my lovely wife. I am so in love. Thank you, Lord, for loving us so much, His extraordinary love, His mystery, undeserved, unknown until He brought it to us. You have unravelled parts of me I never knew existed. I came such a long way to find you, Jayne. There are still things I want to share with you but do not know how to explain, times when I smell a perfume or fragrance in the air when there are no flowers around. Sometimes in our home, there is the softest wave of this fragrance which comes and goes. I am beginning to think it must be the presence of an angel, but I don't know. Then there is music and sound that comes into me that I have never heard before. Soothing, peaceful, it makes my whole self relax. I have no idea what is happening, but I know it is to do with His love for us somehow.

All my love,
David

PART 2

---·◆◆◆◆·---

*T*ouch Jesus, Meet God

From the beginning of our relationship, David and I read the Bible together, prayed, and witnessed together. We sought God's direction for us as a couple and enjoyed a normal family life and an average Christian life. We both had secular jobs; David was an architectural technician, and I worked in the care services.

This would be a good place for me to describe what else was happening in our life parallel to our family life, daily jobs, and worshipping with friends once a week.

David was beginning to have visions, see angels, and have powerful dreams he had not experienced before. He was having supernatural experiences. It seemed these experiences were increasingly linked to our witnessing.

I cannot remember the exact date, month, or even year we decided to take our adventure with Jesus to the next level. We became aware our conversations were increasingly turning towards a desire we both had, to tell others about the loving God we had met and who had made Himself known to us through His son Jesus. The only way of doing that effectively would be to find ways of talking to people who had not yet met Jesus. That meant leaving the church building on Sunday mornings and going out where other people were on Sundays.

We both shared the view that our approach to telling others about Jesus would not be via leaflets or gimmicks – we wanted to get to know people and do something gentle and encouraging, to present an invitation which could be responded to or rejected without offence. David was adamant: he would not use a formula and we would not promote any particular denomination. We would only promote Jesus.

We bought a nine-foot square gazebo (small tent). David made a wooden cross, four feet in height, that we could put into the ground as a signpost to the tent. We called the tent "Touch Jesus Meet God".

We purchased a variety of children's picture Bibles, children's books, tracts, and stickers to give away free, and we asked a church for any used, ordinary Bibles they would also be willing for us to give away free.

The church was very generous. When we went to an event, we piled the Bibles up on our fold-up table and put others in baskets with a sign: "Pre-loved Pre-used Pre-proved" or "Tried and tested – guaranteed". We were ready to take the invitation out for people to touch Jesus and meet God for themselves.

Surprisingly the Bibles went every time – like hotcakes! We were always asking the church for more.

We had approached various event organizers and booked

pitches wherever we could: the Highland Fling, the Norfolk Park Show, the Transport Festival, the Lowedges Festival, Winter Wonderland, the Norton Show, as well as attending car boot sales at weekends through the summer months if there was not an event to sign up for. A friend also offered us her hairdressing salon in the centre of the city for a weekly prayer meeting.

Wherever we could put up our tent, we would, and wherever we were invited, we would go.

We discovered the event organizers were very friendly and very happy to have their pitches booked – a half-empty field is not good business for anyone.

With our diary filled and our Reserved tickets in hand to show the steward when we arrived, we packed everything into our Volvo Estate, and the two of us went out to tell people about Jesus.

There is not room here to tell you of all our adventures and escapades that happened at these events. I can only give you a flavour; we were welcomed by other traders, and many of them asked us to pray for their stalls, their business, their families, and themselves. We discovered an event culture we had not come across before.

The coffee wagon offered us free tea and coffee all day, the hot roast pork man gave us free buns stuffed with hot juicy pork, sage, and walnut stuffing, apple sauce and the most drool-worthy delicious crispy crackling you can imagine. The American Civil War Re-enactment Society were very friendly and allowed us to take lots of photographs of their camp, their soldiers – the Blues and Greys; and their "field hospital". The World War One and Two Re-enactment Society and the French Resistance Cafe were also friendly. Because we were eager to listen to their stories, they were eager to ask us why we did what we did and why our obsession was Jesus. They were asking us to tell them about Him!

There were many other groups we met and talked with, whose spare-time hobby was dressing as Victorians or Edwardians. We met and talked with Gothic Revivalists, individuals, couples, and families who dressed as various characters from well-known films – *Pirates of the Caribbean* and Cap'n Jack Sparrow seemed to be favourites one year. We chatted with Roman soldiers, pagans, and Druids, and we were invited into a chuck wagon belonging to the Pioneers. Any and all historical events and characters, or fictional ones, were represented by their enthusiastic supporters.

There were many not-for-profit charities: the Badger Protection League, the People's Dispensary for Sick Animals, hospice care charities, and many others. The farmers markets were always well attended. The reason I have mentioned these various groups is because in all the years that David and I attended out local shows, fairs, and events, we did not once encounter any hostility.

We were treated as family by other eventers. They knew who we were, and we trusted the Holy Spirit to bring those to our stall, or to initiate conversations with, those who He was already working with. We did what we saw He was doing.

The "Touch Jesus Meet God" tent was used by members of the general public who visited the events when they needed to take shelter in the rain, or should they need to have a sit-down on a chair when they were tired of walking around. Youths would leave their bikes with us to keep an eye on while they went round the stalls or watched amateur groups perform their "thing". Sometimes we were asked to take care of another stallholder's stall while he or she took a break and wandered around the other stalls to chat with friends.

David and I felt as though this was where we were meant to be; this was our place and it was easy.

We had great fun – especially when we put a large sign up declaring, "Free Prayer for Anything".

We also discovered these activities increased our own love for Jesus and our need of Him like nothing else could. I'm not sure if it was the Holy Spirit or the biggest adrenalin rush you can ever know, but we were having the most exciting and extraordinary time of our lives.

We were praying more and for longer before we went out to an event, because we had to trust God in all situations, and we did find ourselves in some interesting situations.

Having initially thought it would be fun to do something by faith and see what God would do, neither of us anticipated this had been His idea all along. He did not let us down, and the supernatural began to invade the natural in ways we could not have orchestrated.

The more we prayed for strangers, the more strangers came for prayer to our stall, and we began to see prayers answered and people being saved. The more free Bibles we gave away, the more free Bibles we were gifted by a local church to give away. We made crosses out of lollipop sticks and stuck them in a bucket of sand with a sign that said, "Please take a cross and write your name on it or someone you would like prayer for, and we will pray now or later." We never had less than fifty crosses with names on, some with prayer requests scribed into them to take away and pray over. We gave regular testimonies to the church who had gifted the free Bibles, and they also backed us with prayer and prayed over the crosses we brought back.

There were many opportunities to pray for people on the spot who had never crossed the threshold of a church building on a Sunday morning.

We thought on many occasions, the fields really are white for the harvest.

> Say not ye, There are yet four months, and then cometh harvest? behold, I say unto you, Lift up your eyes, and look on the fields; for they are white already to harvest. (John 4:35 KJV)

One such occasion, we noticed a man standing with his back to us, watching the show ring where sheepdogs were working. He was with his family but every so often kept looking back over his shoulder towards us. His family moved away from the show ring, but he stayed. Then he began walking to and fro across the front of our tent. This went on for a while; he disappeared and then came back. He walked away and then came back again. This went on for about two hours. We said nothing at all. As tempting as it was, we did not approach him but waited to see what God would do. It was a hot day, so I went to buy ice cream. When I got back David was talking to the man; he had come over a few minutes after I'd left and had said to David, "Is it too late for me, mate?"

David said, "Not today, it isn't," and led him in a prayer to receive Jesus Christ as his Saviour and Lord.

Another occasion, after we had been talking to two young women and praying for them, they asked if they could be baptized in the water. David looked surprised and said, "What water?"

One of the young women looked down and pointed to a large steel bowl of water on the ground. "That water," she said.

We didn't know what to say. We brought the large steel bowl of water with us to every event, but the sign had fallen off. It had said, "Thirsty Dogs Drink Here." We had previously noticed that many people brought their pet dogs to these events, and on hot days, their pets were thirsty. Realizing this, we began taking bottles of water with us to give away. Word had got around there was a bowl of cold water for thirsty dogs at the Touch Jesus Tent, and it was in great demand. We were embarrassed. The two young women had anticipated immediate baptism after they'd received Christ, and we were not ready! Sorry, Lord.

If the water had not already had many dogs drinking out of it, I think we may have baptized them both there and then – like Philip and the eunuch.

> And the eunuch answered Philip, and said, I pray thee, of whom speaketh the prophet this? of himself, or of some other man?
>
> Then Philip opened his mouth, and began at the same scripture, and preached unto him Jesus.
>
> And as they went on their way, they came unto a certain water: and the eunuch said, See, here is water; what doth hinder me to be baptized?

And Philip said, If thou believest with all thine heart, thou mayest. And he answered and said, I believe that Jesus Christ is the Son of God.

And he commanded the chariot to stand still: and they went down both into the water, both Philip and the eunuch; and he baptized him. (Acts 8:34-38 KJV)

Our faith was being stretched as we began praying for people in ways we had not prayed before. We were facing the challenge of spreading the news that the kingdom of God was near to everyone, in a variety of secular environments with a multi-faith or no-faith audience.

But some went away with a new faith and a new friend – Jesus.

PART 3

<hr>

*A*ngels, Dreams, and Visions

As the momentum of our witnessing increased, the Holy Spirit took a hold of David in a deeper way. He began to spend longer with the Lord alone and sometimes seemed quieter in his whole self. Things were changing.

David began to see angels regularly and have visions that he described as three-dimensional pictures about three or four feet in front of his eyes. When I asked him what he meant, He described it as "a bit like looking at a hologram". Sometimes they were interactive. When this happened he could see a moving picture. Sometimes he was in the picture himself at the same time as looking at the event taking place from where he was. David described it as being out of time and in time at the same time!

I apologize if this is confusing; it was for me as well.

David also started to dream vividly, and he said he had never dreamed before in his life or, if he had, did not remember any dreams.

The Lover: There are times when I am quiet in my body, when I am silent and do not talk, times I take myself off into our garden alone, but that is when I am talking with my Lord. He shows me things. We have been brave enough to ask for love. Love is writ in our hearts with a diamond-tipped pen.

My beautiful Jayne, our Lord Jesus is doing something new with me, something new with us. I am not sure what this means. When I am alone with the Lord, I am beginning to see more angels and more vivid visions.

May 2007: Jayne, Katie, and I took Jazz, our dog, for a walk in our local forest today. Jazz was foraging in the undergrowth. Jayne and I were walking along the path. Katie said, "Look, can you see that?" Jayne and I looked around and saw what looked like golden rain. It was not coming down vertically, but coming through the forest horizontally, swirling all around the three of us.

It filled the area we were standing in with what looked like pinhead dots of gold. We stood still to see if we could feel any dampness on our faces and thought it must be rain, mist, or low cloud, but we were perfectly dry. Everything around us was dry.

The dots of gold went up through the tops of the trees and touched the ground as well, like a column. Everywhere we looked, in every direction, the gold dots were around us. We stood still for a long time watching the gold. It was like being in a snowstorm globe but with gold dots that reflected light. We did not know what it was, but it was amazing.

This lasted a few minutes, about three to five. It seemed a long time, but we stood still and just looked around us, expecting it to disappear within seconds, but it didn't. It lasted long enough for us not to be able to dismiss it as rain or fog or some sort of natural phenomenon, because it was not falling like rain. It was around us and when it disappeared it all disappeared at the same time and was gone. We looked to the edges of the woodland to see if it had moved somewhere else, but it had all gone. We did not know what to make of it. We looked at each other but didn't know what to say. We thought it was a lovely gift from God to be able to see and witness something we had never experienced before. We just felt, wow, what was that? Thank you, Jesus.

June 2007: I saw an angel today. Only a glimpse, I believe it was real. Sometimes I seem to be aware of their presence. I am asking the Lord, "Why me? I am not the sort of person who sees angels or has visions." I'm nobody, just ordinary. I am asking the Lord for more, more understanding.

I have had visions for some time now, not regularly, but sometimes He shows me things and sometimes gives me warnings. This morning I woke up, and God showed me clearly the face of a person I needed to avoid.

Later in church, only two hours later, I could see the person approaching us and immediately heard the Lord say, "Get up, get out, and don't look back." We did. The person did not follow. I do not think the person saw us.

The same day, in the afternoon the person came to our home and wanted Jayne to get in the person's car and go for a drive to talk about what they thought God was telling that person about me. Jayne refused.

Sometimes He shows me what is in people. I see their

spirits and other spirits attached to them. Sometimes I have dreams with such vivid clarity I know He has shown me something I need to understand or a place to go to or something or someone either to talk to or to avoid. He is talking to me and saying, this is the way.

When we pray for people, I never know what is going to happen. I trust Him. I am not scared; I just don't know what to make of it. I have shared this with people we know, people I thought would know about this sort of thing, but they don't seem to. So it's you and me, love, as it has always been, on our own, one step at a time.

David always shared his experiences with me (Jayne) and regularly with other Christians. Some of our friends made a fair attempt at trying to understand what God was saying to David. The problem we had was that we could not find anyone who could explain David's experiences with absolute clarity or offer any teaching. Even those who had similar experiences said they could not teach the subject matter. They simply accepted, like David, that "these things happen sometimes". There was no one available for any of us to progress our understanding and relate these experiences to scripture.

1 September 2007: I was admitted to hospital due to an erratic pulse, a spiking temperature, and atrial fibrillation. The doctors could not find what was causing this. Then Kath came to see me in hospital and prayed, and said, "In the name of Jesus, I command this sickness to come out of the darkness into the light." She said, "He's going to be all right. I have just seen two angels by his bed, one at the head and one at the foot."

I knew they were there to protect me and everything would be ok, and it was. That evening the consultant decided to do an ultrasound scan of my abdomen and found a burst abscess on my appendix. Hallelujah, they didn't operate, just drained off the poison and gave me antibiotics.

During my stay, I began to see other angels as well. They were standing around the beds of some of the people.

I saw a golden, sparkling light come through the ward today. It was like millions of tiny flakes of gold, like the gold snowstorm we stood in before. This time I knew it was the presence of angels escorting demons off the premises and out through the window. Angels were healing some people, and they did not know.

25 October 2008: In the Spirit, I am walking down an unmade track with Jayne. To one side (right) are sections of ruined walls, some with doorways and windows. I notice some windows protected with Perspex sheet, very neat fit, a large lodge-type building off to the left at a right hand curve in the path.

I see a circle of people sat inside in wicker armchairs. All are smartly dressed. Jayne goes straight in saying, "I know what this is." I am outside; men and women are confronting me. There are children around about them. All are in Sunday-best clothes.

I am very firmly stabbing my right-hand fingers on their foreheads, saying, "Get out. Go back to where you belong; you're not wanted here." I keep walking, and the people keep coming. I keep confronting and casting out. I am not afraid; I do not want to turn and run away. I keep saying, "Oh no, not more of them" On and on. Jayne is out of the building and back with me.

The demons have gone, and people are as they should be. Calm, there is no fuss and no running around. Three men are sitting on a bench to the left. The middle one leans forward to kiss me. I say loudly, "We don't do that here," and prod him on the forehead with the fingers of my right hand. The person disappears.

We come across more people waiting, but we have cast out all the demons. Then I woke up, came back.

26 October 2008: I woke up thinking I had not had a dream last night, and then almost as an afterthought I remembered the dream. I had taken off my spectacles with my right hand, and the right arm of them was broken; so too was the top right hand of the right lens.

It was broken and cracked in triangular pieces. When I turned the specs over to look at the front, there was a break from top to bottom, but it did not need glue to hold it in place to fix the break. Then I was awake.

Not long after I was in the shower, I understood the interpretation – someone was going to try to break the vision of where God is taking us.

They were going to attack the "right-hand man". This is a warning from God; He has made us aware to be on our guard. Thank you, Lord, again.

12 November 2008: I am in an open vision. An "open vision" is like watching a moving picture in front of me. But it is more than that; it is also like a hologram that I can be involved in and watching myself from the outside at the same time as I am inside the vision. I know this sounds strange. I don't really know how to describe it. I am walking through a demolition site. It is below street level. There are brick retaining walls and other buildings above. These are intact at street level.

The cellar was exposed. In the wall of this demolished building was a glass-fronted two-door case, completely intact. In it were blue and brown smocks and things associated with work. I walked past, came back, and looked, walked on, walked back. I did this three times in all. I wanted a smock, but the door was locked.

Then I saw two men running up to the case. The men started to break the glass. They were trying to steal the smocks; they were trying to steal things that did not belong to them. At the same time, two other figures came running out of a building on the opposite side of the site, shouting to stop the thieves.

A friend gave me the interpretation; the building site represents God taking the church back to its foundations. The glass cabinet with the smocks in it is still intact – not touched, not broken, nothing stolen. God is saying, "I put these in the foundation and protected them." The colour of the coats are significant. Blue is for the priesthood. Brown is for the disciples who were sent out.

The two men who were trying to steal them were coveting the mantle of the priests and the disciples (the coats represent the mantles). It is a warning. The other two figures coming running and shouting – they were God's messengers coming and warning me, "Don't let anyone steal your mantle."

A friend told us that in the spiritual realms, demons will see your mantle even if you are not aware of it. They will try to take it from you or try to stop you using it. Do not let them. They can only work through people if you listen to wrong advice. You only listen to God.

Our friend did not explain what "mantles" are; we understood them to be the gifts or abilities or even a particular task God gives you to do, but you can mistakenly allow it to be taken over by others or corrupted in some way. We may be wrong.

In my dream, I fancied a brown smock; however, coming back from work today, I parked the car and passed some men on their eleven o'clock break, all wearing blue smocks. I guess the colour of my smock is up to God.

19 November 2008: A dream – I was sitting on a carpet, watching jewels appearing in front of me, all sizes, all colours, pale lilacs, citrine, amethyst, sapphires, lots of stones I didn't know the colours of or what they were.

There were others mixed amongst them which looked like large, yellow, emerald-cut stones but I knew these were plastic. I wondered why they were amongst the precious stones. I collected them all up and held them and said we needed to show them to someone who would know the difference.

Then we were sitting on a beach in a small bay. I put the stones on the sand, but I was not worried about losing them. A wave came in and swept around the back of us, it came in front and covered the stones. Some of them disappeared from view.

Then I had a sieve in my hand and stuck it into the sand. I looked and the plastic ones had disappeared. I said, "Thank goodness we've still got the genuine ones. The plastic ones have been separated out."

I looked down and saw a cavity appearing in the sand. I saw other different stones. These looked like very large crystal shapes on fire – the size of apples and pears. I knew these were more important than the ones in the sieve but did not know why. I said, "We need to know the names of these stones, then we will understand why we have them. Their names are the key."

We did not ever think we had a correct interpretation of this dream. The only thing we thought at the time was that it was obviously about genuine precious stones and artificial ones, like costume jewellery, made of paste. We also thought it may have been for someone else to interpret it, so we shared it with friends but no one knew what to do with it. Perhaps there is someone reading this who will know.

November 2008: During a prayer meeting, I had a picture image. I saw what looked like a bulkhead door that separates chambers in a vessel, the door closed, locked fast, and completely sealed off. I asked Dad (Father God) what was behind the door.

He said, "Contaminated water." I then saw into the chamber as though the walls and door was clear plastic.

I looked and saw it filled with murky water; all sorts of debris were floating in it. It had become part of the ocean. I looked around and saw a gaping hole where the dirty water had come in.

The water had contaminated everything inside. The

contents destroyed and were rotten. There was nothing left to salvage.

I asked Dad why the owner of the vessel had not repaired the hole, pumped the dirty water out, and cleaned everything up.

He said, "These are the chambers of their heart. They know they cannot do the job themselves, but they do not trust me to do it for them. They think I did it. Until they want the tear repairing, that chamber of their heart will stay that way. And unless they start trusting me, it will be the same every time. Eventually all the chambers will be filled up with contaminated water instead of my Spirit."

8 November 2008: As I was waking up, I had a picture in my head. I saw a new, strong white canvas sail catching the wind. I want to be the sail that feels the wind pulling and stretching the sail to move the boat.

Then I am on Noah's ark; we are sailing calmly. Our house is on the ark; it is where we live. I am going in and out of the house and sometimes looking over the side of the ark into the sea, looking for swimmers who need to rest, but there is no sense of anxiety or fear.

A friend gave an interpretation: "Your own home will become a sanctuary where you will provide for people."

15 January 2009: A vision – we are running up a mountain stream, bounding without effort from rock to rock, with both feet at the same time. Then we are running up stream higher and higher. This is the stream from the throne room, and it is no effort. Next, I am given a key with three crowns on it, and I am told this is the master key to the building.

29 January 2009: I wake in the night, taken into a Vision. God is lifting Jayne and me up by our clothing on our shoulders. He is taking us to the next level. He said we have been running up the shale scree at the lower part of the mountain – we have come to a wall. He has to lift us up. There is no pressure; He is just lifting us up unexpectedly, No feeling of being pulled or pushed, just lifted.

Next, very early in the morning I woke up and saw a figure in our bedroom, standing beside our curtain wardrobe. He was buttoning up a jacket/coat/smock. I could not tell which. At first, I thought it was Jayne, but she was lying next to me, fast asleep. Jazz (our German shepherd dog) was lying on the carpet, watching but not disturbed. *What is this about, Lord?* There was no fear. Then I know this is an angel and the message is "It is time to put on your blue smock. Get ready to go out."

22 February 2009: Sunday afternoon, Jayne and I are out walking on Ramsley Moor. Jayne is ahead of me, with Jazz running in between us. I feel a definite firm touch on my left shoulder as if someone is reassuring me: "I am here with you and everything is ok." This happened twice within a short time. Peace.

23 February 2009: Monday night, Jayne and I are praying for people at church. The presence of Jesus is strong. One person is receiving prayer ministry and is lying down behind some screens for privacy. I look up and see three abstract-shaped upright figures, a washy-grey colour, without substance, moving across the top of the screens from left to right. The person praying continues quietly. I watch as these spirits move towards the double doors and leave. Jesus sets the person free. There is no noise. Everywhere is peaceful.

I knew that David frequently saw into the supernatural spiritual realms. He saw angels and demons when Jesus made them visible. David was never afraid when these things happened and would wait until the Holy Spirit spoke to him to see if David was to take any action. I did not see anything, but the other person praying did and concurred with David.

Jayne

24 February 2009: Tuesday morning very early, I am aware of a very bright light almost hot on my face and on my forehead. I open my eyes and I look up. Above the top of our wardrobe is a vision of the stonework of lancet church windows with their delicate stone filigree carving clearly visible.

There is a brilliant light burning through very brightly coloured glass panels. They are bright yellow, red, and blue. It is as if I was being reassured about something. I have a vision that I am taken onto the road outside. I am looking up into the sky and see skeins of geese, and I know they are coming back home. They are increasing in number, faster and more and more. What is this about, Lord? Are these the prodigals returning home?

11 April 2009: We have been praying with a small group of friends for our city for a number of years. Early this morning I was half-awake and half-asleep. An open vision appeared in front of me.

I saw a settlement in an area surrounded by hills. There was a group of people firing flaming arrows out of the city towards the prayer house. These people did not want the city saved and were rebelling against God. They were firing warning shots.

As if in an instant, red and yellow traces of light came from the hills to my left side and to my right. These became so many that the sky filled with flaming arrows, like a firework display. There was a deluge of fire across the city.

These arrows were carrying a message to all those praying in the name of Jesus Christ for the city. "Don't mess with us. We are big names." The deluges of incoming arrows were from those who want to remain nameless and faceless. They did not want to be uncovered, and they had tremendous power.

I saw a black mesh cast over the centre of the city to bring in darkness and works of the devil. These were celebrations of the occult. At the same time, a square tower of a church in the city caught my attention. It had four spires. The spires were silver points on the tower corners. As the black net was cast, it snagged on the tower's silver points and was torn.

I wondered why God, who sees all, let the black mesh be cast. It was then that I saw the mesh caught on the four silver points and ripped wide apart. I heard a voice say to me, "If God had stopped the net being cast, the devil would have done his work and taken it away, having a usable net to cast elsewhere. By allowing the net to be cast, it was caught on the silver points and destroyed and could not be used in any other place or city. The net caught on the four silver points rendering it unusable again."

I asked God what were the four silver spires on each corner of the square turret on the church. I was wondering about this imagery. A square turret with four silver spires, I know it must be something to do with *the* church rather than a particular building, but I do not know what.

Some years later, the meaning of the silver spires on each corner of the square turret of a church came; Jesus is the only Saviour, Jesus is the only healer, Jesus is the only baptizer in the Holy Spirit, Jesus is the only returning King. There is no other truth. Prayer will expose the enemy. These four silver spires will render lies powerless.

May 2009: I am walking along a broad earth road. I am caught up in the middle of a royal parade. I see a woman in an old-fashioned riding habit, riding a horse in front. There is a man who looks quite robust, and I know he is a prophet of God. He says he had been carrying something, and it is time for him to pass it on.

He calls me over to him, opens a box, and it has inside highly polished leather tack for all the horses in the parade, bridles, bits, and all sorts of reins, reins for long carriages, and short riding reins. He says, "This is yours." I take it. When I wake, I can physically feel the weight of the box and its contents as I carried it.

July 2009: I am taken into an open vision. Jayne and I are standing on a hill, looking out over into the valley and seeing a city in shining gold. I thought it was a picture of the New Jerusalem at first, because it was a city in glory. However, it was not. It was our city as God sees it, as seen in the heavenly realms. God has a new name for our city. The heavenly name reveals the identity in heaven and the purpose for the city on earth. It is not a name thought of by man; it is not revealed to me. When this prophecy is released, there will be many who claim to know the heavenly name of the city and its purpose. They will say God has revealed it to them. However, the name also reveals the next move of God in the city, and He will validate the name and the purpose of the city by working with them and confirming His word with signs.

David sketched these visions as he saw them. When David had a vision that included me (Jayne), I didn't query it. I accepted whatever the Lord showed him, because I trusted the Lord and I trusted David, I simply thought it was interesting. It never occurred to me to wonder why I was present, because David and I did everything together. It would be more unusual for me not to be with him.

Jayne

7 February 2010: A vision – a 99 ice cream appeared in front of me (this is a rice paper cornet filled with white ice cream and two chocolate flake sticks stuck in the top).

I heard Dad say, "I will give you a double portion."

I said, "Why show me a picture of an ice cream?"

He said, "Because my double portion will be sweet to the taste."

Then I saw a view of the front of our house with a passion flower in full bloom also full of fruits hanging down. There were more fruits than leaves. The flowers were out at the same time as the leaves. I don't know what this means.

May 2010: A dream – I was walking along a road when I realized I had no shoes on. I quickly looked around for a shoe shop to buy a pair of shoes. I went into a shop, but none of the shoes would fit me. I came out again and continued walking barefoot.

I thought there should be a pair of shoes somewhere to fit me, and I wondered why I couldn't find any. I asked God to show me the shoes he had for me.

He said, "I have given you heavenly shoes. You will not find any shoes to fit you here."

7 June 2010: I have a clear open vision of a very large black rectangle nearly taking up all of my eyesight. Then I see countless shining white dots all over it, breaking up the dark. This is an encouragement from Dad to show us we are not on our own, He has people everywhere, many more than we know, shining out for Him.

7 September 2010: Jayne and I have the same vision – to have a place called Psalm 23 where broken people can come aside and rest awhile. For many years, since I first visited Northumberland I have wanted to live there, not just to go for another holiday. I know this is where Psalm 23 needs to be. I became quite emotional about it.

I saw two arms in front of me, holding a paving slab loosely wrapped in a purple cloth. The hands of the giver of the paver were bare, the arms visible to the elbows only. Both of us were covered in long, white cotton garments.

It looked as if the arms were coming out of the bottom of cloud cover, not just one cloud. This image was followed by the right hand, offering me three long, white-handled artist brushes. They had never been used. They were perfect and for our use.

9 January 2012: Early morning vision – our grey/brown/glass mixing bowl has dry ingredients in it. Once mixed with liquid, its mixture is poured into my white pint mug. When we pour the mixture back into the bowl, it overflows and keeps on doing so.
    No interpretation. Is Dad asking us what will we pour out for Him? Guessing.

27 January 2012: We are going to hear a call to go where we did not expect to go. We are in an unusual season. Get ready.

10 March 2012: I had three simultaneous visions from God.

1. Jayne held something in her hand. She opened her hand slowly and out rolled a brilliant white light ball. This ball darted, flew, whizzed around the room. It eventually settled high in a corner, shining its light on us. I have experienced bright lights whilst in bed. The light is so bright it comes through my eyelids. When I open my eyes briefly, it is still night.
2. Again, in bed I saw a portal opening and brilliant white light coming from it. It was getting brighter as it opened.
3. A javelin is released from our Dad God. It is flying past us at unbelievable speed to a city – dead on target. Dad is saying, "I told you I will look after you. Follow the truth." Dad is saying, "I've created a weapon fit for purpose."

25 March 2012: I saw the cross on fire; a river running red dropping as a waterfall into a ravine; red clouds; a leaden grey sky; a chink of light from a door in the blackness; and a figure in the doorway.

I went through the doorway into the daylight; people were wearing bright colours of red and blue; bright green grass; blue sky with white summertime clouds; and I joined with them. The javelin was still shooting by overhead.

9 April 2012: While praying, I had a clear picture of a field on fire. The fire was destroying all the straw and the stubble. This is like Obadiah 1:15-8. It is Esau and the straw is already on fire today. This is our city being cleansed by the fire of the Lord – the word of God.

> For the day of the LORD is near upon all the heathen: as thou hast done, it shall be done unto thee: thy reward shall return upon thine own head.
>
> For as ye have drunk upon my holy mountain, so shall all the heathen drink continually, yea, they shall drink, and they shall swallow down, and they shall be as though they had not been.
>
> But upon mount Zion shall be deliverance, and there shall be holiness; and the house of Jacob shall possess their possessions.
>
> And the house of Jacob shall be a fire, and the house of Joseph a flame, and the house of Esau for stubble, and they shall kindle in them, and devour them; and there shall not be any remaining of the house of Esau; for the LORD hath spoken it. (Obadiah 1:15-18 KJV)

8 May 2012: We are praying and I see a very large angel in white and silver clothing, holding a broadsword. In front of the angel was a row of people he was looking at, but they could not see him. The angel did not speak, but I heard the Lord say, "If they speak lies, their heads will be removed."

2 July 2012: I wake up abruptly; God is reminding me that I recently widened our garden path. We can now walk where we could not walk before. Our path is wider and safer to walk along.

He is going to take us along a path we have not walked before, to fulfil a role we have not thought of. However, it is not yet fully developed.

He is alerting us to changes that He is bringing about. Something new is beginning, and we are not to be afraid.

I see someone coming to attack Jayne with a baseball bat. Jayne is hit on the legs and crumples, knocking her to her knees. Then I see something else. Seconds before I raise my index finger on my left hand and touch the baseball bat, which immediately bursts into flame and then ash.

God says He sees everything. The attack stops. No weapon formed against us will succeed. God has already protected Jayne. Praise the Lord.

22 August 2012: I am live streaming Christian teaching, and as I listen, I lift my hands in praise to worship God. As I do so, my hands begin to tingle all over. It is increasing, and then I feel a powerful swirling of something all over my hands, my palms and around each finger.

It is the Holy Spirit. God is saying I need to pay close

attention to what He is saying to me. He is putting all things under His feet.

As I mentioned earlier, we could not find anyone local who properly understood these experiences, and no one who was teaching about them. Most of the Christians we knew either did not believe signs, wonders, and miracles were for this age or did not believe angels visited anyone anymore, and still others thought unusual dreams were "pizza" dreams caused by indigestion. We could not find a church that embraced preaching and healing as an indivisible commission. Even those who were trying to "have a go" were restrained and constrained by their denominational rules and structures.

In desperation we went online and discovered this was not the case in the United States of America. We discovered ministries whose leaders were capable, willing, and eager to share what God could do and was doing. We began to dip in and out of various online ministries, and as we listened and learned, we no longer felt isolated or peculiar. Our church became other believers who believed, like us, that Jesus is the same yesterday, today, and tomorrow.

17 October 2012: I am on the road outside of our house. It is being resurfaced. In my prayer time, this morning I had a vision, and Dad spoke to me. He said the old tarmac-wearing course (topcoat) is being dug up and removed.

It will not be thrown away but is going to be used as a foundation for a new road elsewhere. What was our topcoat will now be underneath and become the underneath.

Our road will then be given a new topcoat. We are being given a new wearing course. "Our covering, our protecting layer has had its season for us. It is being taken elsewhere to build up others. We are not to be afraid because He is going to give us a new outer topcoat. He is going to provide a new layer of protection and a new road for us to walk on so that we can help others along the road."

24 October 2012: Dad shows me a sign written in bold letters, **"You will not misread this plan I have for you. It states: This Way Up."**

"Tell people it is not too late for them to come to me. Jesus is for everyone. They will find a safe place for themselves and for their families.

"*Feed my sheep.*"

This is the second time God has said, "*Feed my sheep.*"

9 December 2012: I had a vision of being on a railway station platform and jumping up to grab a ticket that was wafting above my head. It was my ticket. There were other figures trying to grab it, but I caught it and held it fast.

As I grabbed it, I felt Jayne's hand touch mine, and it all went calm. All the other figures disappeared. The ticket was blue and had written on it, "Free Admission." It was large, about A4 in size – approximately 8.5 x 11 in. – and was blue.

I heard a voice say to me, "You are buckled up and wearing all my armour under your white robe. You are equipped to stand and to keep standing right up to the end of this war. The victory belongs to God."

9 January 2013: I have a vision of the King in a field in Northumberland. He is saying to me, "I am here to hear my people." We have to present our petitions to Him at the

King's table in a tent in a field. I can see the tent covers the width of the entire field. The canopy has a scalloped edge, fluttering in the breeze.

He is waiting to hear His people's voices. I see a gold coin in Jayne's hand. It has a portcullis on it. This represents heaven's currency; it is a whole crown about two inches in diameter, with a rim.

I hear a voice say, "You will know how to spend this currency. I put a handful of blank gold coins into your hand when you first met me, but you did not know how to use them until now. These are your resources from heaven I have sent them to you. They are gold because they are from the Sovereign. You have joined the King's army. You are called to be sent out."

28 January 2013: I have a fall on the ice on our road. Arms underneath me break my fall. An angel broke my fall.

29 January 2013: Jayne made our bed yesterday and shook out the clean linen sheets. Sometime in the night, I felt something small and pointed under the bottom sheet and had to get out of bed, wake Jayne up, and see what it was to remove it. Underneath, we found a small white plastic dove.

It was one of the white doves arranged on our wedding cake, but neither of us could think how it got there. We had eaten our cake on our wedding day and put all the little white doves carefully away in a box. The bed sheets are kept in the airing cupboard.

I knew God was talking to me and asked what it meant. He said, "It's time for the dove to return to the ark. Your journey over dry land will soon be over." I do not know what this means for us, but praise the Lord.

20 February 2013: I can see Jayne and me in an old railway carriage – green embossed-leather upholstery, mahogany wood fittings. The door on the corridor is part open. I cannot see if there is anyone else in the compartment, but everything feels very safe and comfortable even though we do not know where we are going.

The feeling I get is to carry on doing as you are doing until you get the next set of instructions. Keep trusting Jesus for the journey. Then I hear, "Get ready. You're going over a bridge."

26 June 2013: I have a vision of us unexpectedly facing a wall of stone, the Lord telling us we had strayed off the path He had put us on. We had strayed so easily. We only realized when we came up to a high stone wall. However, there was a way up.

There was a grass embankment to one side, and cut into the embankment were steps. We went up the steps and ascended, rejoining further on the pathway where we should have been. (Thank you, Lord.) The steps disappeared behind us, which seemed odd, as it felt like this was so that no one would be able to follow us.

We walked along the path and went through an open gate and could only see a short way in front, because the path turned a corner we could not see around it. The gate closed behind us – we could not turn back, and no one could follow us. We were not afraid. Our obedience to keep walking forward would change everything.

I saw the following: Katie, my stepdaughter, had made a patchwork quilt and had sewn biblical quotes into some of the squares in gold: "Wherever she is, she will be sleeping under a blanket of prayer."

Joy, my other stepdaughter, was wrapped in a cocoon woven by Holy Spirit: "She is in a safe, secure place of growth and development."

I saw Jayne and me walking along hand in hand in a giant bubble: "I am protecting your walk."

I was praying and saw a young girl lying in a bed. She was in a hospice. She had cancer.

She had turned her face to the wall and was looking at a tree. As she was looking out of the window, a tree was moving through the seasons. She was looking at autumn, and the leaves were falling off the tree one by one.

"Tell her to turn over and look out of the other window. If she looks out of the other window, she will see a tree with new buds on it starting to burst and blossom, and she will get well." I passed this on, but do not know what happened.

24 September 2013: A picture came into my head very clearly of Jayne and me walking together in darkness, but we were walking on gold paving slabs. Each slab was also reflecting golden flashes of light along the path; the flashes were coming from partly open doors along the way.

These doors were set ajar to give a guiding light, but we were told not to go through any of the doors at the side of the path but keep walking and only go through the doors that would be on our path directly in front of us.

These would be the ones that would fully open for us.

Though we did not know how many there would be. Again, keep moving forward regardless of what our circumstances look like. Praise God. He has given us the encouragement and strategy. Carry on keep carrying on.

19 July 2014. Approx. 5.30-6.00 a.m. notes in journal: Angel is standing at bottom left of our bed, clad in silver. Very tall, he was much taller than our ceiling yet not breaking through.

His wings were not feathers; they were like sword blades touching the floor. I asked his name. "Zebulun," he said.

Later I have a conversation with Jayne. "I woke in the night, love, to hear a violent thunderstorm with lightning coming into our bedroom. An angel about eleven feet tall appeared in the room. I knew he must be taller than our ceiling, but he did not go through the ceiling. I do not really know how to explain what he looked like. I asked his name, and he said, 'Zebulun.' I asked what he had come for and he told me something about our future." I am not sure what it means, so I will not record it until I am sure.

Since that time, I am seeing more angels from heaven, nine, ten, or eleven feet tall, their wings like sword blades. I am beginning to see them now almost on a daily basis.

Today I was walking in our garden, and I became aware of an angel standing next to me, all white, his wings folded. He was walking our boundaries with me; he brought a peaceful atmosphere with him.

I am seeing more visions. They appear like a window opening up in front of me, and I see clearly, as if I am in the place I am seeing. There are times when I awake and angels are already in the room, pure white light but not blinding.

I saw a door through the ceiling of our bedroom, and I heard the Lord call to me, "Come up higher." I took His hand and went through into a place where it was bright. That the Lord should come, show Himself to me, and show me into these realms astounds me. I do not know why He is doing this with me, Jayne, love.

He showed me a vision of creation, and we were there. We existed before time began. I watched as He spoke and the whole cosmos came into being. We were in the cloud; He wanted us. He made us, we were with Him, and we were there. He chose us, and nothing can take us out of His hand. I have sketched a very crude image.

13 August 2014: I keep walking by the fishes in our hallway, knowing God is talking to me. I talked to God with Jayne today in prayer. I asked what the Lord was saying to me, and I got the picture of a fishing boat on the sea. Its nets were full both sides, bulging out, covering most of the boat; I assume it is bulging with fish but cannot see them. What does it mean – the net was bulging, obviously full of something – not visible to us – yet?

26 November 2014: Lord, I want more of the open visions and to see the angel Zebulun again. I want to understand the meaning of the blue mantle you put around my shoulders. Show me please. Why have you given them to me? Do not stop, Lord; I need more.

1 December 2014: I am sitting in an oval room faced by a number of highly polished hardwood doors with brass fittings. Each time I push one of these doors, the room inside is empty. None of the rooms has anything in them, and I am afraid to keep trying to no avail.

I then ask Jesus to walk with me and hold my hand. He does. I notice a bright-red painted door with brass furniture, and I am afraid to go through. However, Jesus holds my hand still, and we enter the room. In the room is a gold rod with a curved top. Within this is a gold disc. It is the heart of Jesus, and of course, the rod is His shepherd's crook.

I ask Jesus to remove the heart of stone that is within me. And without hesitation He removes the stone heart and implants the gold heart (the disc from the shepherd's crook). The rod/crook stands in the room, and the gold presence of Jesus fills the place. Jesus takes me once more by the hand, and we walk away from the red door room.

My rock heart has gone, and a gold heart sits in its place. My fear has gone, and I walk away with Jesus with me.

The following is a vision that was given many years ago to a friend of Jayne's. We knew that God was talking to us all, but we did not know what to do. We took it to our church leaders, but it was not understood, and there was not anyone who could interpret dreams and visions. However, at intervals through the years, the Lord has repeatedly brought it to mind more powerfully than before. It has come back again.

The Lord: Gather the stars.

The Lord: Bring me the stars.

Me: What are the stars, Lord?

The Lord: The stars are my messengers and my worshippers. Bring me my worshippers, and I will unlock the wells."

I think the plan is bigger than we two.

PART 4

+·+◆+·+

Captivity and Deliverance

By now, we had become used to the supernatural realm being a part of our natural lives. We normalized it, but we did not understand it. We did not know of anyone in any local church who could unpack this with us fully or who was teaching a Christian perspective on the interface of heaven and earth and the supernatural realms from a personal experiential position.

There was nothing in either of our previous religious church backgrounds, whether it was Baptist, Methodist, or House church that had preached or prepared us for what was happening to us and particularly to David.

For example, what do you do when an angel comes into your bedroom during a lightning storm and gives you a message? Or when you feel Jesus closer than ever before and He talks to you, warns you about an event that is due to take place in less than two hours, and then instructs you when to leave?

So we did what we always did, continued to walk out our walk, trusting Jesus' love for us, knowing He keeps His promises. As David often said, "We're on our own, love, just as we always have been," meaning none of our friends seemed to know what to make of our experiences either. We did not know at the time that we were about to find out how much our trust would be tested.

The Lover:

11 February 2015: I feel a small lump on my right-hand groin. Our friend, Paul Swift, prays for me. Paul heads up a Christian ministry called Closer to God. He is a close and trusted friend. He put his hand on my side, and I feel a cooling on my skin and over my body. I feel healed of something.

19 February 2015: I become ill with stomach pains. They increase, and I am doubled up. Jayne calls the emergency services. An ambulance arrives, and I am taken to hospital. An assessment is carried out, but they are unable to diagnose a specific cause. I stay overnight.

23 February 2015: The pain returns and I am admitted again at 5.30 a.m. for observation.

26 February 2015: An angel appeared in the room, wearing a brown (unstitched) garment. I felt peaceful – he had brought peace. A second, larger angel appeared, dark-skinned, goatee beard, Ethiopian looking. He wore a blue tunic. He asked if I was cold and if I would like a blanket. He had one with him.

He covered me with a biscuit-coloured blanket. It looked like smooth, flattened horse hair. I felt warm and fell into a deep sleep, and the angel disappeared. I was woken at

8.30 a.m. for breakfast. The blanket had gone – disappeared. About noon I was told I was being discharged and my case was being managed as an outpatient.

27 March 2015: Angels are around me on a daily basis. I was walking in our garden today when I became aware of a figure dressed all in white at my side, not speaking, just walking. It then dawned on me – He was walking our boundary, with me. Thank you, Lord.

17 April 2015: Dad (Father God), walk with me daily in order to restore my soul. Dear Lord Jesus, I surrender my soul to you. I invite you and welcome you to put your soul into me. "David, spend half an hour simply doing nothing."

I believe God healed me when Paul prayed for me and I felt the coolness on my skin. That was God's word and promise. Be it done to me, as I believe. The rest is processing the promise, working it out, because I know my healing has already taken place. This is my testimony to Jesus – it is finished.

22 April 2015: I am admitted to hospital for an assessment. I am diagnosed with an aggressive cancer throughout my bowel, intestine, and stomach. They believe it is not possible to remove it, as it has spread too far. I am told they will operate to undertake a bypass to the large bowel, but if they cannot remove the cancer, and that if I died on the table, I would not be resuscitated.

23 April 2015: I underwent surgery. My body was opened up and closed up again with twenty-three steel staples in a neat vertical line up the length of my abdomen.

The bypass was completed successfully, but the cancer mass was still present as the surgical team had been unable to do anything to remove it. My consultant told me that whilst I had survived the operation, which they had not expected, their next assessment was that I had only two days to live.

I survived the two days, and when the consultant visited the intensive care unit a second time and discovered I was still alive, he amended his prognosis to two weeks at most, due to the aggressiveness of the cancer still in my body.

I must admit I thought it was a miracle as well. I thought I had died during surgery, and I remember having a conversation with Jayne when I came round. I said to her "Am I dead?"

She said, "No."

Then I said, "I think I died."

Jayne said, "You did not die, darling."

Jayne had brought my prayer shawl and laid it across the bed.

3 May 2015: Paul came to the hospital to pray for me. Jesus appeared in the room. When Jesus showed Himself to Paul in the room, it was to grant us a testimony to all present so they could say it was for others and us as well. Jesus said, "It is finished."

Emails:

On Saturday, 9 May 2015, Jayne Burgin wrote:

Hi Paul, this is going to sound a bit off the radar, but I was using David's Bible yesterday and found an old prayer he had written. I cannot write it out in full here, but what I seem to be looking at in these present circumstances is God answering. Not sure where I am going with this, but suppose God puts a seed in our bloodlines that he purposes our bloodline will fulfil, a sort of God DNA that glorifies His name, not just a biological DNA. This can be halted or diverted by generational sin and/or our own.

But when we receive the Holy Spirit we trigger that spiritual DNA to life again to fulfil Gods purposes for our family bloodline, and in the same way we break curses from previous generations, we can call back blessings and works God intended our bloodlines to fulfil and release these in our generation.

I think this is what David has done without knowing. What we are going through is somehow linked with David restoring a bloodline blessing in obedience to God and in answer to his prayer; it is a sort of flushing out what should not be there and a renewal of Gods original plan for His purpose and us.

David wrote something about realigning the times, and for him to come into Gods realignment, He asked God to change the times and reverse all of the effects of generational sin. The prayer is not dated, but it's old paper, so it is some time ago before all of this. He ended it, "So that your will be done on earth as it is in heaven." Any thoughts?

Blessings,
Jayne

On Monday, 11 May 2015, Jayne Burgin wrote:

Hi Paul, I know you have a lot of stuff going on. I wondered if it is possible for you to come over to the hospital again one evening and anoint David and pray, this time to pray over David's stomach. We had a difficult meeting today, and we had to listen to all the negative stuff again. When we got back on David's ward, he was exhausted. He asked if I would get in touch and ask if you would be able to come over. I know we do not have to receive any lies from the devil, and we pray every morning at home. I pray over David during the day, and me and the girls do it again at night. I still believe when you saw Jesus in the room, cancer left. It was not possible for it to stay in the presence of Jesus.

Blessings,
Jayne and David

Paul to Jayne Burgin, 12/05/15

Hi Jayne,

I was planning to come over again anyway. I just need to sort out the rest of my week but aim to get over later in the week possibly Friday again. I am refusing to accept anything said. Personally, I never give up on the word of God.

We know God does the healing and we know we have the authority as his children to declare the truth and change the natural. He makes all things new.

Another interesting point is how every time I have planned

to come to see David this week, others around me have fallen ill. I am determined that I visit early next week and between now and then will seek the Lord for further revelation.

I believe declaration of the truth by many of us will spoil the trap and rout the enemy from their plan.

Blessings, Paul

Jayne Burgin to Paul, 14/05/15

Hi Paul, I agree with everything you say because Jesus has also been talking to David and to me separately. Just too much to put in an email.

Blessings Jayne

17 May 2015: David – The Lord interrupted my prayers and said, "This is important. Bring to mind the word 'emerald', and you are to speak in the language of precious stones not words or images. When a man touches a stone and puts it under water it loses its edge because the film on a man's fingers dulls the stone. Even if they polish it or buff it up, it will still be smeared with the residue of their fingers, because they have handled it, but I am coming as a diamond with a language for my own creatures."

He is not coming back to interpret the message again as though it was given to animals, having been translated by humans. This translation is for humans not to be translated by humans. "When the world gives a gift it diminishes over time, but when I grant something, the gift granted is forever. Out of my generosity, I issue to you all the fruit this field will produce."

When David wrote this down it did not mean anything to him at all. In fact, he wondered if it could make any sense to anyone. However, he shared it with a friend and as soon as he mentioned the word 'emerald' the person knew exactly what it meant and understood how it applied to him. The only indication of meaning he felt he could share with us was a scripture reference, 1 Peter 2:4-8.

I obtained permission to put this entry into David's book because it was so unusual and gives an example of the importance of delivering a word faithfully from God without tampering with it. It does not matter if the 'postman' cannot read the letter – he isn't supposed to, as long as the recipient can!

> To whom coming, as unto a living stone, disallowed indeed of men, but chosen of God, and precious,
>
> Ye also, as lively stones, are built up a spiritual house, an holy priesthood, to offer up spiritual sacrifices, acceptable to God by Jesus Christ.
>
> Wherefore also it is contained in the scripture, Behold, I lay in Sion a chief corner stone, elect, precious: and he that believeth on him shall not be confounded.
>
> Unto you therefore which believe he is precious: but unto them which be disobedient, the stone which the builders disallowed, the same is made the head of the corner,
>
> And a stone of stumbling, and a rock of offence, even to them which stumble at the word,

being disobedient: whereunto also they were appointed. (1 Peter 2:4-8 KJV)

20 May 2015: My high God, high God, what have I left behind? I know what I have left behind; I have left behind the cancer. Amen. Glory to God. I have to stay in hospital to recover fully from the major operation.

21 May 2015: It is as though my hospital room has become a tabernacle of God. A tent or a meeting place, it is a little piece of the Kingdom.

Paul comes whenever he can. Joy and Katie are here every day and stay at night. We sing and worship. It has been a real joy to see my sons. I look out for Jayne as soon as I wake up. Jayne comes every day, all day and the evening, until she is asked to leave for me to sleep.

During the daytime, we have had so many people ask about the Bible on my table, nursing staff, care assistants, the domestic staff who clean my room every day. Even one of the members of the surgical team came to see me, because he was amazed I had survived as long as I have, given what he saw in my body during the surgical procedure and could not believe I was still alive.

Some have shared their own faith in Jesus, and this is a real encouragement. We have talked and prayed with people and prayed for people telling them about the goodness of our loving God even in these circumstances. The hospital chaplain is a treasure, a real gift from God, a genuine brother in Christ.

Talking about Jesus gets a mixed response. It is sad; some do not have any hope for eternal life in heaven with Jesus, even for themselves. After the last meal of the day, the girls

(Joy and Katie) come for the evening, and we sing songs and worship.

On Friday, 22 May 2015 Paul wrote:

Hi Jayne,

Yes, we need to keep praying and declaring I completely agree and "every cell" is a good word as the cells were relevant when we prayed together. I will tell you in a few weeks or when the Lord says the time is right. I will plan to get over after the weekend to pray with you all again if that's ok.

Keep me informed for prayers.

Many blessings,
Paul

To Paul, 27/05/15

Hi,

Results of MRI brain scan:

The consultant came and talked to us and said there is no brain damage, there are no brain bleeds, and there is no evidence of any brain tumours and no cancer cells in the brain. They thought he may have had a stroke but have cancelled that out as well. They cannot find any evidence or any abnormality in the brain. They are beginning to wonder how he is surviving.

Blessings,
David and Jayne
Hallelujah, Jesus!

Paul to David and Jayne Burgin, 27/05/15

Amen, God does a complete work.

I agree with Katie's vision. I was going to reply and say just wait until he walks out unaided, because I saw the same thing, and then I read what she had seen. I also see him coming to churches with us and lighting the fires. (David's testimony used to light fires of revival) All for God's glory.

Blessings,
Paul

During David's hospital stay, we experienced problems to do with the level of care being provided. I talked it over with Paul later and asked him to pray.

Telephone call to Paul from Jayne (27/05/15):

As you know we have been having some problems at hospital. They are still unable to provide a bed which is long enough to accommodate David due to his height – six feet three inches. His feet always stick out at the bottom of the bed, and he tries to curl himself up at night to keep his feet warm. Unfortunately, the bed is not very wide, so before I leave at approximately 10.00 p.m., I raise the rails on each side of the bed to prevent his rolling out of the bed during the night. Unfortunately, the rails have been lowered repeatedly every night by night-care assistants, and David has fallen out of bed on at least three occasions. I saw this recorded in his notes that were hooked over the end of the bed. I continue to complain about this, but I have been told it is hospital practice to lower bed rails during the night.

Email from Jayne Burgin to Paul, Wed., 27/05/15

Hi Paul,

An update for you about yesterday, David saw four doctors in the morning, and one came to see me in the afternoon. They would not discharge David today as planned, and they have said they now want to do a deep bone scan on Thursday, so the earliest he could be out is Friday, but we are not sure. Following the MRI scan on his neck, they say they can see two points of lesion on his neck bones and want to investigate further. The cause of these could either be due to a trauma injury from his falls in hospital at night when he was alone or more cancer cells. They are not sure which. I am asking the Lord to heal David from the marrow in his bones outward. I have recorded all the things the Lord has revealed that He has healed. I believe God is continuing to heal David slowly. I have asked for every attack against David to come out of the darkness into the light, that there is no hiding place for the enemy. This is what I see is happening. These are the things revealed so far.

- Death is overcome.

- We were told David would not survive the operation and that they would not resuscitate him. David survived the operation.
- We were told David only had two days to live following the operation. David lives.
- We were told David had two weeks maximum to live. David still lives.
- Cancer is dead. It was in his small colon, intestine and stomach, now they are looking for it in his neck bones and brain. They have not found anything.
- There are no cancer cells in David's neck.
- Later the same day, three consultants came and confirmed to me again, there are no indications of cancer in his brain. Praise the Lord.
- They expected kidney failure; it did not happen.
- They expected David's heart to fail; it did not happen.
- They diagnosed permanent visual impairment. It did not happen – that's a ha-ha funny story. Nobody thought to ask David if he wore glasses when they were assessing his eyesight. The visual impairment was because he was not wearing his varifocal spectacles. As soon as his spectacles were given to him, his eyesight was back to normal.
- The multiple chest infections that were recurring cleared up.
- Two urinary tract infections have cleared up.
- The oedema is resolved. It has not returned.
- The expected liver disease is not there.
- All blood disorders have cleared up; he has no current blood disorders.

- Suspected hidden pneumonia did not manifest.
- David's blood pressure is stabilized.
- The other infections they found; which I was told was caused by the cannulas (identified by a care assistant who noticed a vein in David's arm changing colour to purple); resolved when they gave him antibiotics.
- The consultant said David currently has no infection in his body. Moreover, he can now be discharged from hospital, hopefully 1 June.

They would not offer any follow-up appointments as an outpatient or any treatment for cancer.

I am praying ongoing healing for all the work of the enemy to be bound and sent to the judgment seat of Christ. David said, "I don't think anymore. I pray." Katie had a vision David would walk out of hospital fully healed without assistance and with his head held up with a group of people around him. Perhaps this is taking longer than I anticipated because God is doing a greater work.

Blessings,
David and Jayne

During the time David was in hospital recovering from the operation, we had some wonderful moments talking about Jesus to some of the evening nurses. When most other visitors had left, Joy, Katie, and I sang praise songs at David's bedside. Other patients had their radios on, so we knew we were not disturbing anyone. One evening we were singing softly because David was asleep. A nurse came into the room and said she had heard us singing. She told us she was a Christian and asked if she could join us for a few moments. Of course we said yes. She was from a Pentecostal Church. While we were singing, we heard a quieter sound and realized David was singing with us. He said he had been dreaming and could hear us in his dream and wanted to join in. The nurse brought us all a cup of tea and biscuits. It was a very special night.

On another occasion, a representative from an organization that specialized in supporting families at home who have a family member diagnosed with a terminal illness came to talk to David and me in David's room. The woman was very pleasant, very polite and professional, but behaved as though David could not understand what she was saying and spoke to me the whole way through. I don't think she addressed David once. Unfortunately, I didn't do her much good either, I'm afraid, because the moment I began telling her we were Christian, we were not afraid of death if it should come, but neither would we engage with her in a conversation which seemed to assume death was going to happen within hours of our returning home. We were not planning a funeral. I asked if she had a faith at all or what her particular belief system was. What did she think happened when we died, and if she believed human beings had souls and spirits?

Sadly, she did not believe in any kind of life after death, and I thought how difficult it must be for her to support families with terminally ill relatives when you could not offer them anything of substance. She could not tell them about God or Jesus or Holy Spirit. She could not support their grieving with a hope that would last forever and by which they could see beyond the death of their loved one to a time when they would be reunited. How lonely.

Jayne Burgin to Paul, 28/05/15

Hi Paul,

I asked the Lord yesterday what *He* is doing in this.

When I went to hospital during lunchtime, a young man came in to dry mop the floor. He picked up David's Message Bible and said, "What's this?"

I said, "It is a Bible. Have you ever read one?"

He said, "Only at school but I like to think I'm open-minded."

Me: "What are you?"

Young man: "I'm agnostic."

Me: "What's that?"

Young man: "I'm open-minded about God. I don't believe he's an old guy with a long white beard sat on a cloud."

Me: "Neither do I, but are you open-minded enough to say, 'If you are real Jesus, show yourself to me'?"

Then followed a conversation, which was extraordinary. He stayed asking me questions for about forty-five minutes. Eventually he said, "I hope you did not mind me asking you all this. It is something to think about."

So we are praying for this young man as well. That is two people who have come into the ward and conversations about Jesus have happened. So I think part of the wait has to be that God has people He wants to talk to and when He has finished bringing the people into David's room that He wants to get their attention, and then it will be time to leave. I know David's times are in the Lord's hands as well. In the meantime, we keep on fighting, because we will not be slaves to fear.

Blessings,
David and Jayne

To David and Jayne Burgin, 01/06/15

Hi,

I am praying for David's release today. God told me next time I see him is at home.

Amazing that it is forty days. I feel released to share something today because we refuse any death sentence from oncology. Do you remember when I asked you about the door, when you were with David in his room in hospital and the door was banging and I discerned the wind, but then I became aware of death trying to get in? The Lord showed me to pray and refuse it access, just as you have been doing, and to declare life. I know death has been refused access, and therefore anything else is a lie we need to shrug off.

I was only having a conversation with the Lord yesterday about James, and I like how he spoke to you too on James. I agree everything below with you sister. I come into agreement and today declare victory and release home.

Blessings
Paul

This next email is the email Paul is referring to above – 'everything below'

To Paul Swift, 01/06/15

Hi Paul, this is the last day of the testing and trial. I realized last night that David had been admitted to hospital on the evening of the 22 April and is leaving during the day of 1 June. That is forty days and forty nights exactly. The number forty is used 146 times in scripture, with God proving His people via trial and testing. Lots more to tell when we see you. In the meantime, we continue to pray even for the last day. This is when we see oncology, and we are not going to accept a death sentence on the last day.

We are praying for the Lord to strengthen David's faith as He promised and that his faith will not fail him. David's faith has certainly been tested during these days, and it has not failed him. I can hardly believe his upbeat attitude.

I am praying like this:

- Failure is not an option.
- Do not only say we have faith, but also act as if we believe it.
- Believe and see what God will do.

Blessings
Jayne

And the Lord said, Simon, Simon, behold, Satan
hath desired to have you, that he may sift you as
wheat:
But I have prayed for thee, that thy faith fail not:
and when thou art converted, strengthen thy
brethren. (Luke 22:31-32 KJV)

The oncology appointment confirmed that they would
not be offering any appointments, and David was discharged
immediately. We all arrived home in the afternoon of 1 June.
Thank you, Jesus.

1 June 2015: I survived the initial two weeks, and despite
having to remain in hospital for observation longer than
I hoped, I am looking forward to being discharged from
hospital today without any further appointments.

From being admitted on 22 April to 1 June, I was in
hospital forty days and forty nights – what is that about,
Lord?

The diagnosis is still inoperable cancer. I have been
advised there is not any alternative treatment which would
change the prognosis. I understand the consultant expects
me to die shortly. I am not given any follow-up appointments.

During my stay in the hospital, I incurred other health
problems. The Lord gave me the strength to overcome them.
(I must admit there were times when I felt "parked" in a side
room.) I was not offered any medication or treatment for
cancer at any time. My understanding was that medication
would only be administered if it were believed it would
enhance the patient's condition. Given the consulting team

genuinely believed I would die within days, there seemed little point. I understood that the nature of intervention (i.e., chemotherapy or radiotherapy) would not enhance my situation, but rather cause further distress. I accepted this and decided to wait and see what God would do.

While I was in hospital, the Lord protected me from kidney failure, heart failure, impairment of my gross and fine motor skills, visual impairment, chest infection, hidden pneumonia, multiple urinary tract infections, drop-neck syndrome, oedema, liver failure, and other infections.

These symptoms may or may not be connected with the cancer diagnosis. I do not know. Nevertheless, when it was time to leave, I walked upright out of the hospital unaided, with Jayne at my side and without a wheelchair, without a walking frame, without crutches, without any aids at all and without any adaptations needed to my home, and without further appointments. Case closed.

I am growing stronger and feel good. I collected our car from the garage, and I am driving again. We are revisiting all our favourite places. I continue to see angels about me, and I am looking forward to telling people about my Saviour. My testings that have been tested are over and have become gold and silver. Jayne, you are my beautiful wife, sister, lover, and friend. What a journey. We are still going strong, love.

At this point David was not offered hospice care. We were not offended by this, and David would not have accepted it should it have been offered. I was in good health; our two daughters Joy and Katie had moved back home temporarily, choosing to commute to their jobs. David wanted to come home, and we wanted him home. He had been through so much, and the three of us felt capable and able to meet all of David's health and care needs between us. We had an excellent local general practitioner and district nurse service who we knew we could call any time for help.

5 June 2015: Dad is talking to me. He said, "Tell people: don't come to me with a list of problems. Come to me for the answer. I have the tools for the whole job, start to finish. It is no good saying, 'I've got a problem, and I think this is the answer.' If you want my answer, sit down and listen to me. I can help you but only if you give me everything."

Man goes to God with prayers like blunt chisels, a wrong-size head on a screwdriver, a saw loose in its handle which causes injury. Go to God and hand it all over to Him saying, "It's bigger than me." He will answer you.

Recognize when some prayers have been said, done, and answered. Move on and ask God for the next prayer, because there are prayers waiting in heaven backing up and waiting to be prayed so that He can answer them with a new dynamic of power.

There are prayers, which already have their answers waiting; some are directional, telling you the way to go. When you can pray, "God get your glory out of this situation," you have a heart at peace with God.

Thank you, Jesus, that during my time in hospital you never left me and sent your angels to help me continue to worship you when I was feeling weak. Thank you, Lord Jesus. My hospital room became like a tabernacle of God, a tent for people to meet you, a tiny portion of the kingdom on earth. Hallelujah.

July 2015: I feel the Lord has put it into my heart to undergo an immersion for a new journey with Him, a mikva. For anyone reading this who does not know what a mikva is, here is my understanding, with apologies for any misunderstandings, especially to my Messianic brothers.

I identify myself as joined to my messianic brothers in Jesus Christ. I lean to my Jewish inheritance, as a Gentile believer in Jesus Christ, who is the Messiah of the whole world. According to the teaching in scripture, it has always been the intention of God to join Jew and Gentile as one new man in Him. See Ephesians 2:11-22 (KJV).

David and I primarily viewed our spiritual identity as it is laid out in this passage.

> Wherefore remember, that ye being in time past Gentiles in the flesh, who are called Uncircumcision by that which is called the Circumcision in the flesh made by hands;
>
> That at that time ye were without Christ, being aliens from the commonwealth of Israel, and strangers from the covenants of promise, having no hope, and without God in the world:
>
> But now in Christ Jesus ye who sometimes were far off are made nigh by the blood of Christ.
>
> For he is our peace, who hath made both one, and hath broken down the middle wall of partition between us;
>
> Having abolished in his flesh the enmity, even the law of commandments contained in

ordinances; for to make in himself of twain one new man, so making peace;

And that he might reconcile both unto God in one body by the cross, having slain the enmity thereby:

And came and preached peace to you which were afar off, and to them that were nigh.

For through him we both have access by one Spirit unto the Father.

Now therefore ye are no more strangers and foreigners, but fellowcitizens with the saints, and of the household of God;

And are built upon the foundation of the apostles and prophets, Jesus Christ himself being the chief corner stone;

In whom all the building fitly framed together groweth unto an holy temple in the Lord:

In whom ye also are builded together for an habitation of God through the Spirit. (Ephesians 2:11-22 KJV).

Because we saw ourselves as grafted into God's covenant promises to Israel, by faith, when we learned about the practice of immersion for different stages of a person's walk with God, we were both intrigued and wanted to know more. Having researched the practice, we saw no reason why we should not incorporate it into our own walks with God. We wanted to honour God and His chosen people.

The Lord Jesus Christ was born a Jew. When He was baptized by John in the Jordan, He was not being baptized into Christianity or any denominational church organization with full-membership privileges. Neither was He being baptized into Judaism. There had to be something else.

I believe a part of the explanation for Jesus undergoing baptism by John was for a public witness to acknowledge the next stage of work He came to do. It was at this time that the Holy Spirit came and made Himself visible in the form of a dove resting on Jesus and the voice of God was revealed to some of those present.

We listened to some teaching that explained that John belonged to a sect of immersers (*immersion* and *baptism* both mean "washing") who were regularly immersing people on a daily basis to separate themselves publicly from a previous walk or role in life to follow God into the next walk with Him, this act was a symbolic demarcation into a new role they believed God had called them to. Hence, the act of immersion or baptism was a public witness that they were washing off their previous walk with God and emerging from the waters into their new calling. The act of immersion symbolized leaving a previous work behind for the new.

John was immersing people symbolically in water to prepare them for the coming Christ. Jesus would baptize His followers in the Holy Spirit to follow Him.

I gave my life to Jesus Christ and was baptized in water by full immersion on 26 February 1984. This represented my decision to follow Jesus Christ as my personal saviour and Lord.

I was later baptized in the Holy Spirit. Hence, my next immersion does not invalidate the first; it is simply a symbol of my recognizing a call to begin a new walk with

Jesus, a symbol of my progressive discipleship – different immersions for different stages.

I have asked my friends Paul and Neil to help with this. Paul made all the arrangements, and I am very grateful to my friends for their love and support to Jayne and me.

My immersion took place during the Feast of Tabernacles, 15 Tishri 5776 (28 September 2015). A friend of Paul's owns a farm and has installed a plunge pool in one of his barns – this was the perfect place.

During my mikva, Paul and Neil spoke prophecies over me.

Neil: You have a message. You have a supernatural ability to speak in public, to speak in private; you will have clarity of thought, completely open to the prompting of Holy Spirit. You will never have to rehearse, because God will put the words into your mouth. Your mouth will open, and God will speak through you.

You will see and hear like Jesus more than you have ever done before, and He will show you into a world that you have never seen before. He will give you a glimpse into the spirit world so that you will see what is going on around you and around other people. You will be a man so full of words from God and prophecy that you will change their lives.

They will hear your story, and you will touch their stories and change their lives. This is declared in the name of Jesus.

David, you are welcomed by God into a new season, and I declare what the Lord has shown to Paul, that your story is a testimony to multiplication for healings.

Paul: And I speak out what happened in the church when the testimony was read out, that two people were healed of cancer.

I declare what the Lord has said: you are going to go into new places as He has said. You are going to speak unprompted. You are going to declare your testimony, it is going to bring an anointing of healing over people's lives, and I declare there will be more cancer healings and more healings of other ailments.

Father, completely anoint David in this new season, Holy Spirit that You fall on him in a fresh way. You fill him with Your words, with Your wisdom, with Your revelation, with Your discernment in all these situations. That you would quicken him; strengthen his body and that you would walk before him in all of these places. We declare new season over you, David, in the name of Jesus.

I see a picture of coals on a fire, and they are glowing red-hot. We blow on them as a symbol of the Holy Spirit blowing, and you will start to burn for Him. Fan the flame in Jesus's name. Hallelujah, amen.

David in the immersion pool with Paul and Neil

Feast of Tabernacles, 15 Tishri 5776 (28 September 2015)

Paul speaks prophecy over David

Neil speaks prophecy over David

Afterwards, we shared a feast and tucked in to roast lamb, apples, honey, halva, dates, figs, grapes, olives, walnuts, boiled eggs, grape juice, challah bread, and red wine. Neil brought his shofar – a ram's horn that is blown to make a musical sound. He blew it loudly, and we all praised God.

PART 5

✦✦✦✦✦

*M*isunderstandings,
Confusion and Revelation

With the events of the early part of 2015 behind us, David driving again, and the prophecies given at his mikva, we both felt ready to "rock and roll" with God again and concentrated on building David's strength up and praying over the next steps God wanted us to take. We joyously celebrated David's supernatural survival and shared his testimony with anyone and everyone who would listen. Our faith had been tested and tried so what was there to worry about. What could possibly go wrong!

We prepared for Christmas, bought the presents, put the tree up, lit the house, and baked. God had been so kind to us, and we couldn't wait to shout about it in the New Year.

The next step was not what we expected or one that I could accept.

24 December 2015: I am admitted once more to hospital. I have been vomiting repeatedly, and it will not stop. It feels as if I am vomiting my insides out, which I probably am.

I have been assessed and diagnosed with fluid on my abdomen, which needed draining. Due to the Christmas period and shortage of nursing staff, this procedure will take place over several days. I settle in to wait. Angels are flanking me. I think about our dream of using our home to fulfil a prophecy of Psalm 23, a place for broken people to come for restoration in Jesus.

> The LORD is my shepherd; I shall not want.
> He maketh me to lie down in green pastures: he leadeth me beside the still waters.
> He restoreth my soul: he leadeth me in the paths of righteousness for his name's sake.
> Yea, though I walk through the valley of the shadow of death, I will fear no evil: for thou art with me; thy rod and thy staff they comfort me.
> Thou preparest a table before me in the presence of mine enemies: thou anointest my head with oil; my cup runneth over.
> Surely goodness and mercy shall follow me all the days of my life: and I will dwell in the house of the LORD for ever. (Psalm 23:1-6 KJV)

I (Jayne) do not know what our dream for Psalm 23 will look like in the future, but for the moment, I remember and hold on to it in faith and the prophecy that was spoken over David by Neil Grant at David's mikva.

"They will hear your story and you will touch their stories and change their lives."

My prayer is that this will happen, because I know Jesus will personally meet everyone who wants to meet Him. Though I have learned not always in the way we expect!

I have not let go of David's vision or the hope I can make it happen.

30 December 2015: Our daughter Joy arrived early in the morning while I was sitting with David. She went to the restaurant inside the hospital and began to pray. Later she said, "I was talking to God and saying, 'I don't know how to pray about this Lord because what I am seeing is that it looks like David is getting worse not better.' Then a verse popped into my head: 'For we walk by faith not by sight.'"

"I looked it up 2 Corinthians 5:7 (KJV) and read all around the passage – chapters 4, 5, 6. Certain passages stood out for me: chapter 4:7-18 and chapter 6:9-10.

> But we have this treasure in earthen vessels, that the excellency of the power may be of God, and not of us.
>
> We are troubled on every side, yet not distressed; we are perplexed, but not in despair;
>
> Persecuted, but not forsaken; cast down, but not destroyed;
>
> Always bearing about in the body the dying of the Lord Jesus, that the life also of Jesus might be made manifest in our body.
>
> For we which live are always delivered unto death for Jesus' sake, that the life also of Jesus might be made manifest in our mortal flesh.
>
> So then death worketh in us, but life in you.

We having the same spirit of faith, according as it is written, I believed, and therefore have I spoken; we also believe, and therefore speak;

Knowing that he which raised up the Lord Jesus shall raise up us also by Jesus, and shall present us with you.

For all things are for your sakes, that the abundant grace might through the thanksgiving of many redound to the glory of God.

For which cause we faint not; but though our outward man perish, yet the inward man is renewed day by day.

For our light affliction, which is but for a moment, worketh for us a far more exceeding and eternal weight of glory;

While we look not at the things which are seen, but at the things which are not seen: for the things which are seen are temporal; but the things which are not seen are eternal. (2 Corinthians 4:7-18 KJV)

As unknown, and yet well known; as dying, and, behold, we live; as chastened, and not killed;

As sorrowful, yet always rejoicing; as poor, yet making many rich; as having nothing, and yet possessing all things. (2 Corinthians 6:9-10 KJV)

"I thought that bits were interesting, because they sum up how the world sees our situation, but not what the truth really is. There's a reference in 2 Corinthians 4:13, "We having the same spirit of faith according as it is written, "I believed, and therefore have I spoken; We also believe, and therefore speak" (KJV). I wanted to know who said this. The reference given was Psalm 116:10. I looked this up. It said,

"I believed therefore have I spoken: I was greatly afflicted" Psalm 116:10 (KJV). If you read the whole Psalm, it's all about deliverance from death."

30 December 2015: I arrived at hospital at 9.30 a.m. to meet David coming out of the shower room, a bright smile on his face and happily telling me he had just had a lovely breakfast of orange juice, porridge, toast, and a lovely big mug of sweet tea.

He was waiting for the consultant to complete his rounds, to find out when they would be completing the procedure for draining the rest of the fluid from his tummy. The care assistant left the room.

David lowered his voice, drew me close to him, put his arms around me, and said the following:

"The Lord told me this morning, love, I wouldn't be with you for much longer. I am going home, love. I'm going home. I am so very proud. I'll always love you. There's an angel. He's waiting."

I answered that I did not want to hear this, it could not be true, I did not believe it, and I could not see an angel. This was a body blow; it felt as if I was being kicked in the head, punched in the heart, chopped at the knees, all at the same time. We had come through so much. No. No. No. I would not receive this. But I knew David had never lied to me. He only ever spoke truth.

David sat on the edge of the bed, caught his breath, and started to gasp quickly. I ran out of the room to look for a nurse. I found one. She followed me and attended to David immediately. She called for the doctor. He came in and put the oxygen mask on David's face.

He called for other doctors; they came. In all, there were about ten or eleven doctors in David's room around the bed. David was now lying on the bed, propped up, and drawing breath as fast and as deep as he could. A senior nurse took my arm and tried to encourage me that it would be better if I waited outside while the consultation was taking place – not a chance. I remained holding David's hand, stroking his forehead, and telling him I loved him.

This scene continued with no let up through the rest of the morning and afternoon and into the evening. Numerous doctors came in and out of the room, and eventually, sometime during the afternoon, the diagnosis was made that David had a blood clot on a lung.

The decision was to try to dissolve the blood clot via an injection of an agent to thin the blood. It was administered direct into his tummy. The procedure was undertaken, but it made no difference. I asked for a bed to be made up in the room, as I would not be leaving.

Night came with no relief for David. He was looking tired, having struggled all day and now into the night, trying to find a slow, deep breath, but none came.

At intervals, he took off the oxygen mask and repeated, "I love you," and I stroked his hair, kissed his cheek, saying, "I love you too, my darling. Don't you dare leave me. This is not the plan."

This was how we spent the night hours.

About 1.30 a.m. David started to talk to Jesus as though I was not in the room. He spoke quietly and I could only see his lips moving. I knew he was not talking to me, because he was not looking at me; sometimes his eyes were open, sometimes closed, and now and again I heard Jesus's name. I did not want to listen in to such a private conversation this was truly a Father-and-son moment – but I could feel in my spirit David was getting ready to leave. This had never happened before, and I do not how to describe it.

It was the next day, 31 December 2015, 2.05 a.m. I watched and saw a golden light hover over David. Then David was saying, "Jesus, I draw from your power," repeatedly.

The golden sparkling light entered his tummy, he breathed out, and as he breathed out, the golden light left and disappeared from my view.

I knew I had seen the glory of God. I felt as if God had let me see what it looks like when we change in the twinkling of an eye. He came to collect His son David, and David went with his Father. I have no doubt he was flanked by angels, 2.05 a.m., 31 December 2015.

I knew God had permitted me to see this, but I did not know at the time why. I cannot fully explain it, but I knew it would be important for me to remember later on, so I wrote it down.

I was numb. When I eventually read what Joy had been reading on the morning of 30 December, I could not find out who wrote Psalm 116. However, it seemed to me that the message of the scriptures that Joy had been reading, when put together, was that as Christians, even though our faith may be tested to the point of death, we will be given the strength to endure even this trial and that our testimony to others will be that our faith did not fail us even in death. This is because we have the Holy Spirit within us which is the guarantee of our eternal inheritance, though this is not seen or understood by the world. I believe that when we receive Jesus Christ as our Lord and Saviour and ask Him to come and live inside us, then He puts inside us the same love, the same faith, the same light that Jesus had with the Father.

The love and faith and light that Jesus put in David did not fail David. And David did not fail his Lord.

> For God so loved the world, that he gave his only begotten Son, that whosoever believeth in him should not perish, but have everlasting life. (John 3:16 KJV).

PART 6

.•◆◆◆•.

More Revelation, Still *Do Not Know the Plan*

When you lose your love, there are no words, because there is no feeling. There is nowhere you belong. You are utterly pole-axed, your soul feels dislocated from your spirit, and you don't care. I didn't. I prayed every night for Jesus to take me as well, and every morning I woke up disappointed. I cannot take any credit for coping and arranging what had to be arranged and dealt with. Our daughters did it all. Bless you, Joy and Katie.

On 20 January 2016, we sold the first print of the watercolour of Rose Cottage to someone in Florida, USA. It was posted on 22 January 2016, the day of David's "Au Revoir" service.

Paul, our friend and brother in Christ Jesus, gave thanks to God for my beautiful David. He wrote David's message for his au revoir service:

David was a loving person, deeply full of love for others and full of God, a lover of Jesus, Yeshua, a lover of Jayne, a lover of his children.

He was constantly writing notes of love and adoration, pouring out his gratitude and imparting a revelation from God when he was given a vision.

David was constantly in communion with God, increasingly aware of God's presence and heavenly host with him.

He desired one thing – truth – the truth and simplicity of God, Father, Son, and Holy Spirit, and he looked for this truth in his pursuit of God's will for himself, his family, friends, and church, a truth that had never been tainted or distorted by people's opinions.

Throughout all the trials of his life, he always forgave, he loved, he reached out, and he accepted those that were unacceptable.

In every direction he travelled, he looked for God, and then he set out to walk in that direction in faith.

He was married to Jayne, and he partnered with Jayne in all aspects of his life. They worshipped together, prayed together, ministered together.

Jayne was God's gift to him, to walk together down those avenues of life, loving others, speaking the truth, not wavering in God's work, together walking in faith, lovers of each other, lovers of God, lovers of Israel, and lovers of others.

He never tired standing out in fields in all seasons, all weathers, with a tent, which he called

"Touch Jesus Meet God", inviting people to know the God, whose love never failed.

In his walk with God, David identified with Israel and God's plan for "One New Man". He was looking forward to the future and whatever God planned for him would be ok. Therefore, I want to offer what David would offer – an opportunity to know the one true God and His son Jesus Christ.

If there is anyone here who does not know Him and would like to know more we can talk later. Let's bow our heads and thank God for the life of David. Amen.

Days later, I still did not believe what had happened – shock, trauma, disbelief, incredulity, all the textbook processes of grieving. But where was God in this? As valuable as our medical professionals are, they could not help me with this. After all, death is the world's plan. Death is not the kingdom plan. David had lived nearly a year after being told he was not expected to survive the operation and was not offered any cancer treatment. He had survived supernaturally.

I thought I had reached my capacity for anger at all enemies of God: of illness, sickness, disease, infirmity, and death. However, I was now facing the prospect of having to contemplate life without my David. I had not anticipated one final breaking. I had to make the journey to the funeral directors to collect David's ashes alone.

The woman at the funeral directors was compassion itself, but she could not reconcile me to this last act of love only I could perform for David – the retrieval of David's remains. The administration completed, I walked out of the building, and as I looked up to heaven, my heart, my spirit, soul, and body, every fibre of my being, screamed out loud to God, "Jesus, Jesus, Jesus, where are you? No woman should have to carry her husband's remains home in a green plastic jam jar in a carrier bag! Where are you?"

I walked home very slowly and deliberately as though David and I were strolling arm in arm again through the valley up to the top of the hill, then stopped, and sat down on the bench that overlooked our east-facing allotment patch. A turquoise sky was festooned with gold-orange ribbons of dusk falling over the town. I tucked the green plastic jar even closer under my arm and thought, "Well love, we've never done this before. How long do you think I'll have to stay here before I'm allowed to be with you and what on earth happens now?" The arrowhead of my compass home had disappeared. I placed the jar on my lap, held it to my breast, crumpled over, and cried.

PART 7

✦✦✦✦✦

The Other Plan Unfolds

W hat happened next to Katie was a real curveball. I did not doubt her experience but did not know where to fit it in my knowledge of scripture and experience with Jesus so far. Nevertheless, I kept on searching until the intellectual locks in my brain began to tumble and I realized that Jesus had already set a precedent for Katie's experience when He appeared to His disciples after the resurrection. Jesus was taking us all now even further into kingdom reality. But we were so very slow to join the dots between scripture on the page and living it out.

See what you make of it.

Katie's dream vision, May 2016

I was in my room. I could see out of the door to the top of the stairs. I glanced up as Mum walked past into the bathroom and as she went in, I saw David suddenly at the top of the stairs.

He sat down on the top step of the quarter landing with his back against the wall and he looked at me and said "Hello" as if he knew I was surprised to see him, as if it had been a while – like when I would come back from Leeds. He was smiling and there was a glow around him, or from him, like when sunlight comes through a window.

As I saw him I was so excited and I started to shout to Mum saying "David's come back to visit us," but as I did he faded away as he could not stay. Then in the dream, I was still sat in my room and I tried to imagine David again sitting there, but I knew it was just my imagining and the memory, or image, of David in my head was different to how he had been when he sat at the top of the stairs.

My memory of him, he was older, but when he was sitting on the stairs; his hair was blacker and I did not remember him wearing glasses. As if he was a younger man than I remember but it was still David as if I knew him too, he was not unfamiliar.

I (Jayne) asked Katie to look at some photos we had, but she had seen David younger in her vision than she had first known him – which was when he was forty-six years. Katie said David looked very different to David at forty-six years or even sixty-eight years.

It was as though God had drawn back the veil and allowed David to appear to Katie as he is in heaven now, young again and healthy. It was David as Katie had not known him on earth, it was David before Katie and Joy became his stepdaughters.

David no longer looked his earthly age, his body no longer bore the scars of being ravaged by cancer and he looked about his mid thirties. Raven black hair. A big smile, a lovely 'Hello'. Thank you Jesus.

So why is this important? Because seeing beyond the veil is sometimes permitted – Jesus initiated it. He showed Himself to His disciples when He resurrected.

He went on showing He was alive; look it up. In Matthew 28:1-20 (KJV). Jesus demonstrated the separation between heaven and earth is over through him. The kingdom of heaven is closer than we think.

God gave David dreams, visions, prophetic words and permitted him to walk with angels – as David says, "on a daily basis." He wrote these down and shared some of them with me. However, there were many more not recorded, nor shared here.

Because we believed God was talking to David, we did not doubt or question the validity of these experiences. Consequently, neither of us fully understood what was happening to us, we saw no reason to question God.

Hence, I am unable to offer any answers or insight as to the meanings of the few examples I have shared. I have no teaching to offer or theories and I have no new revelations of wisdom. David simply recorded them as they happened to him, assuming similar experiences happened to every Holy Spirit filled Christian. Most of the time, we had no interpretation for ourselves. We did not always think to apply them to our circumstances.

According to Holy Scripture, I believe I live in the last days before Jesus returns. I pray, "On earth as it is in heaven," but I often fail to understand the things I see taking place around me as being a part of this prayer. I live my life day by day. I think this is because I expect "on earth as it is in heaven" to manifest on a grand scale, like some vast fierce eruption in the sky. (I think that is the second coming of Jesus)Yet somehow, I also believe heaven is breaking out into the earth all of the time, and as it increases, it changes the atmosphere when I pray. It changes my perspective of time from a future reality to today's reality. My brain is fuddled by this, it's just too big for me to grasp.

I ask myself the question, how does heaven, which is out of time, break out into earth, which is in time? How do they interlock? Because they are doing so, right now. I used to puzzle over this. I am beginning to understand what this means for me. It may be different for you.

Jesus has not only redefined my relationship with God, He has redefined my understanding of time and space. His love for us increases, it cannot decrease.

That God should have known us before we were born and planned our days, entrusting David's heart into my hands, knowing my flaws, is the most wonderful of all trusts to me. To have been given David to cherish for a short time before the Lord called him home is something that continues to cause awe and wonder to rise up inside. David loved me perfectly for me. David chose not to see my flaws. He never did.

David chose to see me with the eyes of Jesus. He filtered my weaknesses through his love for Jesus and his love for me and saw me as spotless. He looked into my soul and caused me to feel that he saw only flawless beauty.

That is where I found acceptance, joy, delight and wonder. I looked into his eyes and saw unconditional love looking back at me.

Eyes that look into our soul and tell us "you don't have to apologize for living anymore because I see you as you were created by God to be and you are flawless" are Jesus eyes. For me, this is love without measure. No longer measured to try to find where I would fail to measure up.

I know our hearts are safe in God's hands. I continue to read and reread our love letters to one another. My beautiful David, my husband, lover, brother and friend, one day we will sit and read them together again. One day we will start writing another book together in heaven.

"I sat inside the cloud of creation; watching as the very foundations of the cosmos were being laid and we were there. Stars, rocks; all used by God in creating the cosmos. Jayne and David sat with God watching creation and the cosmos being formed."

Even before we were a part of creation, we were in God's heart and mind waiting to begin our serenade on earth and then return to the Father of lights. David.

I think, somewhere deep inside, hidden in a secret place in her heart every woman wants someone to see her inner beauty and to love her. To cherish and nurture her as God created her to be loved and every man I think, wants someone who can see the hero he was designed by God to be and love him as he was always meant to be loved, as he has always desired to be loved.

I think we can choose to see each other as God sees us. We can choose to see with our spiritual eyes. To see into the soul of one another as Jesus sees us. That the eyes of love are the eyes we look into and find acceptance, joy delight, awe and wonder, looking back at us without judgment, condemnation, malice spite or pride. Eyes that look into our soul and say you do not have to apologize to me for anything. I find no offence in you; you are flawless. These are beautiful eyes.

Aren't these the eyes of love? Aren't these lovers' eyes? To know as the Father knows us. To see each other as He sees us, without weakness of character, defect or shadows in our personality. Without remembrance of things done wrong or things not done. To regard one another as having no flaw, as though we have never hurt one another is a beautiful thing to practice. I think this happens when we choose to let Him grow our hearts. I think when we let Him grow our hearts; He opens our spiritual eyes as well. We look into the hearts of others and see no sin. I think this is how the kingdom breaks through into our world. I think this is how we can cause things to be "on earth as it is in heaven."

I heard someone somewhere say, that we manifest on earth, what our souls are in heaven. I apologize for not being able to attribute this wisdom to its original author. I think it is a beautiful truth and I cannot wait to be with David again and others, whose heart desire is to be at peace with God, at peace with themselves and at peace with all others. Get ready, the King is on His way back.

O LORD, though hast searched me, and known me.
Though knowest my downsitting and mine uprising, thou understandest my thought afar off.
Thou compassest my path and my lying down, and art aquainted with all my ways.
For there is not a word in my tongue, but lo, O LORD, though knowest it altogether.
Thou hast beset me behind and before, and laid thine hand upon me.

Such knowledge is too wonderful for me; it is high, I cannot attain unto it.

Whither shall I go from thy Spirit? or whither shall I flee from thy presence?

If I ascend up into heaven, thou art there: if I make my bed in hell, behold, thou art there.

If I take the wings of the morning, and dwell in the uttermost parts of the sea;

Even there shall thy hand lead me, and thy right hand shall hold me.

If I say Surely the darkness shall cover me; even the night shall be light about me.

Yea, the darkness hideth not from thee; but the night shineth as the day: the darkness and the light are both alike to thee.

For thou hast possessed my reins: thou hast covered me in my mother's womb.

I will praise thee; for I am fearfully and wonderfully made: marvellous are thy works; and that my soul knoweth right well.

My substance was not hid from thee, when I was made in secret, and curiously wrought in the lowest parts of the earth.

Thine eyes did see my substance, yet being unperfect; and in thy book all my members were written, which in continuance were fashioned, when as yet there was none of them.

How precious also are thy thoughts unto me, O God! how great is the sum of them!

If I should count them, they are more in number than the sand: when I awake, I am still with thee. (Psalm 139:1-18 KJV)

PART 8

The Plan Unfolds

The Beloved:

My sweetest David, like a half-remembered dream
and a half-imagined kiss,
An invisible warm embrace, on an evening such
as this
When the candles burning low in the silence of
the night
A memory returns and a dream turns on the light.
A rose that could not open without the lightness
of your kiss,
A journey longed to travel but never dared begin
Until you came and took my hand and bid me let
you in.
With clouds of fire dancing, an evening warm
entrancing,
You came to me enchanting in the quiet
evening air.

I am not sure how I arrived here or how long I will be able to stay in this place with you, the place where we are, the place of perfect love, and perfect peace. So I will fill this time, our time, with memories that cannot be spoiled or stolen, that cannot be damaged or destroyed, because they are our own memories, mine and yours, my darling David, our memories of shared first times – the first time we listened to the dawn chorus together and to the last blackbird at twilight perched on the highest point of the beech tree at the bottom of our garden; my wonder at you knowing every birdcall and recognizing every traced outline in the sky when they were on the wing; our memories of summer flowers, heady roses, honeysuckle releasing her perfume on warm summer nights, golden sunlight, silver starlight, romantic moonlight, and safe, warm, cosy firelight with guttering candlelight as we sipped a glass of homemade elderberry wine, together, my love, as we were meant to be; of long walks, cloudless skies, chattering streams, of long, slow, deep rivers; of everyday things, of shopping, paying bills, working on our allotment, choosing our hens for the garden, choosing our pet dogs, buying our first wood burning stove and toasting crumpets and chestnuts on it; even frying eggs and bacon in a cast-iron frying pan over it; making our own wines and laying the bottles down for two years to wait for their slow maturing; pickling shallots and making jams; watching the television together, your favourite Formula One motor racing, golf, and cricket.

We loved listening to Radio Sheffield in the morning and classics at night; buying our first computer and first mobile phones together; putting our portfolio of watercolours together; sharing our home with missionaries who could not get home for Christmas; starting our own evangelistic efforts with a nine-feet-square green gazebo, which we called "Touch Jesus Meet God" and registered for yearly events: the Highland Fling, the Norfolk Park Show, Winter Wonderland, the Norton Show, Lowedges Festival, the Transport Show; and most of all worshipping Jesus, praying for people, standing in fields and festivals with a tent witnessing to the love and glory of God, of the love of His son, Jesus Christ of Nazareth; seeing people healed, set free and offering a welcome chair, for someone who was weary to sit down, and invite him or her to come aside and rest awhile.

I recall our excitement when we celebrated our first Shabbat at home, singing, worshipping, enjoying our favourite foods, drawing a line from all things that had passed into yesterday, and looking forward to the things God would show us next week, where we would go, whom we would meet, and what we would do. How excited we were to have our own prayer shawls, a shofar, and our own Shabbat candles and a beautiful menorah to light.

My darling David, I remember every separate day as though it was today. I can see our beach holidays, visits to National Trust properties, and English Heritage sites, and feeling proud of having Chatsworth House and Haddon Hall on our doorstep. We visited them all so frequently, strolling across their estates, picnicking on the riverbanks, collecting soft wool that had fallen from sheep or had caught on a thorn, imagining all the stories the land could tell.

I recall with clarity the times we enjoyed a glass of homemade port wine in the long grass of our own wild garden, listening to our 1940s wind-up portable "picnic" gramophone record player. We loved listening to old Bakelite records of Bing Crosby, Vera Lynn, and Kay Star. Then along came the Beatles, and David laughing at me because I still swooned over the song "Puppy Love". I knew all the words.

I am so blessed to have so many beautiful memories: gathering fruit in season and trying to beat the blackbirds to the raspberries, blackberries, and strawberries; collecting apples, harvesting gooseberries, pulling rhubarb, gathering plums, cutting mint, rosemary, chives, and continually checking the fig to see if it had fruit – and it did, beautiful big, brown turkey figs.

I recall with a warm glow staying up all night, talking about our pet loves and hates, feeling like teenagers again, raising Joy and Katie together. I so loved that you loved them as you loved your own sons, adopting them into your heart and laughing when you said, "Don't little girls have high-pitched squeaky voices!"

To giggle together, laugh together, to play card games whilst listening to the driving rain beating down on the top of the caravan roof, sounding as though marbles were being thrown at us as it rocked, shook, and swayed in the wind, we played games of Monopoly, Scrabble, snap, dominoes, and cribbage.

All these memories are as sharp in my mind as though we returned from holiday only yesterday, to sit at your feet, resting my head on your knee, feeling your fingers stroke the nape of my neck. I love you, my darling David.

My atmosphere is your atmosphere, David. Our atmosphere was always peaceful and loving, not having to strive at love, simply living in the atmosphere of love. I remember the night of your mikva, your determination to pursue whatever the Lord showed you, our friends celebrating with us. I feel the atmosphere of you when I am falling asleep and I imagine you whispering into my soul, "I love you, Jayne."

As I drift, my eyelids closing, I fancy I feel the lightness of your touch again on my shoulder, a feather-light kiss on my forehead, stroking my hair, telling me everything's going to be ok, sweetheart. It is good to remember our quiet moments, sweet memories and tender words. Love gives all and receives all. Love is a sweeping panorama of fierce delight. There is nothing else love can do but to give itself away and to give itself away and give and give again.

I cannot thank my God enough for giving me the gift of my beautiful David. He used to say he was always in awe of the things God showed him and frequently said, "Why me, Lord?" I knew why: David was an ordinary man with an extraordinary capacity to steward love and raise me to a place where in his eyes, I was always his beloved and in that elevation caused me to meet the God who calls His beloved the bride of Christ, your loving wife, Jayne.

I will not pretend to understand the mysteries of God, and I will not presume to understand why events turned out as they did, because I am still in love with David. I miss him and make no apology. He is still my tall, raven-haired, beautiful husband. God deeply loved David and called him home. Too early for me, but I do not doubt, not a day too early or a day too late for Jesus.

Thinking about love – I've found no matter how much

and how often I tell Jesus how much I love him, or the things I do that I think will please Him, He always seems to do something in my life that shows me He can top that for me every time. I cannot out love God.

Shortly after losing David, my GP felt I could do with a thorough medical assessment consisting of blood tests and examinations involving all sorts of women's stuff. All the tests came back negative. I am, unbelievably, normal. There was one last small thing he wanted to check, my blood pressure.

The health assistant cuffed me with the blood pressure sleeve, pumped it up, looked at the monitor, looked again and a look of panic came over her face. She tried the other arm in silence, and just when I thought she was going to have a go on an ankle, she got up and said she needed to talk with the doctor and left the room. "This is not going well," I thought. It is a little disconcerting when you feel the health assistant is going to have a panic attack. She came back and advised me my blood pressure was 217 over something, which apparently suggested I was at risk of a heart attack.

She said the doctor would be writing to me. I was given a cuff to wear for twenty-four hours at home to see if this was a one off, but no, my blood pressure remained at 217 over something for twenty-four hours. Next, I received a letter in the post, concerned about the situation with a prescription.

In all this time my response to the Lord was "Father, does anyone really think I'm bothered about staying here when all I love is with you? My girls are saved; they each have their own powerful close relationship and intimacy with Jesus. There is nothing in the world I want, desire, or am chasing after. There is nothing I have need of here. Why would I want to stay? I am not desperately pursuing anything; neither am I driven by anything. I've given up trying to work out any plan."

In Christ, we are dead already to this world; we are already living from an eternal perspective. I am happy, Father, if you take me in thirty years or in the next thirty seconds. It is all the same. Your will be done.

I have not left David behind. He is in front, waiting, and he is already a part of the cloud of witnesses. I believe David is healthy and has finished his race successfully. I do not know if David completed all the work he wanted to do for God on earth, but I do know Jesus completed all the work he wanted to do in David's life. Is that the same?

So next, as it appeared I was not going to be taken home immediately, I said to the Lord, "If there is anything I can finish off to complete for David, I'll pick the baton up. Let me carry his mantle, and I'll carry that with my own, even though I don't know what my stuff is." He had said to David one night, "Feed my sheep," and David painted the picture.

Perhaps that was the plan.

So given my thinking that my own heart is now well and truly in heaven, not on earth, I still did not understand the Father's love. Then, spontaneously, He healed me. My blood pressure is back to normal. I am not on medication. He decided to heal my physical heart without my asking. Now, whilst I did not want to be ungrateful to God for this unexpected turn of events, I still have no idea, from my perspective, why He has done this, but He has.

Last Tuesday I visited a friend for a "Jesus Social". We

talked about Jesus and about our ongoing walks to try to understand God's ways. We talked with Him and listened to what He was saying to each of us separately and together. She gave me the reassurance I needed, that Jesus was ok with where I was. He knew.

My friend also said, "I don't know if you will be able to receive this yet, Jayne, but He has just dropped something into me for you, so weigh this and check it out with Him yourself. He says you need a heart transplant; you gave your heart to David. David's heart is sealed in Christ. Your heart is sealed in Christ. Trust Him to take care of both of your hearts. Now He (Jesus) wants you to receive His heart. Will you let Him put his heart in you? Will you steward His heart for Him, and let Him restore your heart?"

Me: "Ok."

She went on. "I can see Him weeping with you, and His tears are falling like teardrops of golden oil into your heart, teardrop by teardrop by teardrop."

I replied, "This is going to take some time; tears falling one by one take a long time to fill a cup." Some healings are slow because they need to be.

I know I didn't earn His love or complete a work to make it happen for me. Some would even argue I didn't deserve this, given my not being bothered whether I stay on this earth or go to the kingdom full time. I still have no idea what He has for me. There must be something for me to complete I have not discovered yet, but I am not arguing over that anymore.

I know again how much Jesus loves me. His love is continually changing me. I know there are going to be times when I fail Him, and that is ok, because all He is truly asking of me is, will I continue to trust Him?

"Jayne, will you trust me when you don't understand and you can't work out the plan for yourself?"

That is all I need to do: to trust even when nothing makes sense. And that is all I need to share, tell people about the love of God in Christ Jesus forever, encourage everyone to love one another, deeply and genuinely. Perhaps those drops of golden oil in my heart are already starting to take effect. Thank you, Lord.

As many others have commented before me, we are spiritual beings simply clothed in physical bodies. Only this outer shell crumbles and decays. My real self, the "me" of me, the "us" of us, transitions through one form into another. I believe we transform, as the Bible says, from one glory to a different and a better glory, laying down mortality and picking up immortality. I know this. I have seen it. I watched the golden cloud fold over David's body and lift as a golden fire made of trillions of particles of gold that covered and hid David's form from my eyes. If I had blinked, I would have missed it. This is my primary evidence, eyewitness account, testimony to the power of resurrection life in Jesus Christ of Nazareth. Yeshua Ha Mashiach. David has entered his rest just as Jesus promises.

12 July 2016, 11.30 p.m.: I lay down to sleep, I was falling deeper and deeper into that peaceful state where tiredness itself falls off one's shoulders, I remembered what David had said: "And when I speak words of love to you, they are from heaven; wherever you are they will reach you, you will hear them in your heart." When I read God's word, that happens. The same peace enfolds me. Thank you, Jesus.

I have learned the gift of a soul created by God, to love, cherish, and care for during their stay on earth is an unimaginable trust, a trust more precious than gold. To discover that your own soul is created by the same God and has been given into the hands of another for the same care and love expected by you for them seems to me to be the value behind loving your neighbour as yourself, and your spouse as your own flesh.

Tell each other regularly of your love for one another. Remind each other Jesus loves us, because the King is on His way back.

It does not matter to God what your personal background or history is. It does not matter how educated you are or not. It does not matter one jot if you are rich, poor, powerful, or anonymous. Your social success, financial wizardry, age, size, looks, culture, or ethnicity are not what life is all about. The only thing God is after is your trust. He is engaged in a relentless pursuit of love for you. He knows we can experience the most life-changing relationships this world can offer; the most radiant romance possible with another person; or spend our lives looking for the "one".

Sometimes we may feel life events and circumstances have short-changed us. God created us to experience life and love in all its fullness, but life is not fair. He knows we strive and struggle, succeed and fail, climb and fall; all the while He is waiting for us to give Him a go. He has a heart cry as well; it goes something like this: "I am your perfect love. I made you to be with me. Give me a chance. I promise you will not regret it."

If you want to respond to Jesus' personal invitation to you, but you don't know what to do, get a Bible to read God's word for yourself. Here are some passages you may want to have a look at:

> Thou art worthy, O Lord, to receive glory and honour and power: for thou hast created all things, and for thy pleasure they are and were created. (Revelation 4:11 KJV)

> For all have sinned, and come short of the glory of God. (Romans 3:23 KJV)

> For the wages of sin is death; but the gift of God is eternal life through Jesus Christ our Lord. (Romans 6:23 KJV)

> For Christ also hath once suffered for sins, the just for the unjust, that he might bring us to God, being put to death in the flesh, but quickened by the Spirit. (1 Peter 3:18 KJV)

> Blessed be the God and Father of our Lord Jesus Christ, which according to his abundant mercy hath begotten us again unto a lively hope by the resurrection of Jesus Christ from the dead. (1 Peter 1:3 KJV)

> He that believeth on the Son hath everlasting life: and he that believeth not the Son shall not see life; but the wrath of God abideth on him. (John 3:36 KJV)

If all that sounds a little overwhelming, it simply means God is the creator and ruler of the world (Revelation 4:11), we have all rebelled against him (Romans 3:23) and because of our rebellion, we all deserve to die (Romans 6:23). But because God loved us so much, he sent his son Jesus to die in our place, then raised him to life again (1 Peter 1:3 and 1 Peter 3:18). If we repent of our sin, that means admit that we were wrong and ask God's forgiveness, and believe that Jesus died to save us, we will be forgiven and we will have eternal life.

If you believe this, then you can pray and tell God that you believe it. Say sorry to him for what you have done wrong, ask his forgiveness and ask his Holy Spirit to come and be with you always.

No matter what you think of yourself or what anybody else thinks of you; you are worth loving – you are worth dying for.

It does not matter how we start with Jesus, as long as we do start. It's how we finish that matters; it could be your day to choose today – don't miss out; I would love to meet you in heaven and listen to your story.

David and I shared something wonderful, as many others do. We are not unique, but we wanted to share our story with you, to encourage anyone who has lost someone they love and who does not know Jesus to find out about Him, because death does not have to be the end of your story. It is not the end of our story. This is why we have chosen to share some of our most treasured moments, even though they simply did not last long enough.

Eventually in every relationship, no matter how beautiful, how pure and lovely, there will always be husbands and wives, partners, parents, children, and best friends who lose each other because separation through death is the end of life in this world. There are as many endings as there are beginnings. But it does not have to be this way.

None of us can avoid physical death. Most of us adopt the world's ways to stave off dying as long as possible. We may choose commercial drugs or homeopathic remedies or both. Surgical procedures may lengthen our stay. We search for the best means of staving off this cursed fiend as long as possible.

Sometimes, saddest of all is the suffering of those who feel there is no other way to protect themselves and those they love from further suffering than to run at death and take their own lives, as if this somehow brings a means of controlling or defeating death. It does not. This does not conquer or defeat death at all. Death only wins when we stop believing in life.

Sometimes the Lord heals physically and completely, and I have heard that sometimes people are raised from the dead for a time. Nevertheless, eventually all of us live in bodies subject to decay. Jesus is the only one who conquered death.

For those who die believing in Jesus Christ as their saviour and Lord, there is peace of mind in death.

The world does its best to help us cope with the process of coming to terms with death. It offers the best support systems, the kindest professional and voluntary services in every field and relationship need. Eventually they fail, because all systems are human-made. They are as human as we are. They cannot promise us permanent restoration with those we love, or reunion, or offer us a perfect eternal relationship with anyone. They cannot guarantee that we will never suffer loss or separation from those we love, and they cannot protect us from the sorrow of losing someone we love.

Humans, on their own, cannot deliver the gift of eternal love. Even though I reread David's love letters to me and mine to him, not one of all our beautiful memories could cease the decaying of his body nor raise David's flesh from the dead. Contemplating a future without David and the love he brought into my life was not possible. I found I could not and cannot handle closure on love, because that is not what God promises. I cannot move on and leave David behind; it does not make sense.

God has promised me something profound. He has promised me life and love in all its fullness now and later reunion with those I love. So how is this possible? Trust Jesus is who He says He is and will do what He says He will do. Simply believe God keeps His promises.

I know David is not dead. He is alive because Jesus is God of the living, not the dead, and David simply trusted Him enough to commit his heart, soul, mind, will, body, and spirit into His hands – everything, his life and his death, trusting in the promise of resurrection life for any who believe in Jesus name.

God's love in me incorporates David's love for me. I feel it. I feel God's love, and I feel David's love. It is tangible; it has substance. This is not part of the loss and grieving process. It is a part of the living and receiving process promised to me by God. This indescribable love is not my imagination. God is simply keeping His promise.

To my lovely wife Jayne on your birthday.
May this be a day of smiles and happiness, all day long. We've been through some stuff love and we've still going strong. Praise the Lord. Thank you for loving me so much. I so love you. Happy Birthday with all my love. David
XXXX And I so love you too! XXXX

We've been through some stuff, love.

These words spake Jesus, and lifted up his eyes to heaven, and said, Father, the hour is come; glorify thy Son, that thy Son also may glorify thee:

As thou hast given him power over all flesh, that he should give eternal life to as many as thou hast given him.

And this is life eternal, that they might know thee the only true God, and Jesus Christ, whom thou hast sent.

I have glorified thee on the earth: I have finished the work which thou gavest me to do.

And now, O Father, glorify thou me with thine own self with the glory which I had with thee before the world was.

I have manifested thy name unto the men which thou gavest me out of the world: thine they were, and thou gavest them me; and they have kept thy word.

Now they have known that all things whatsoever thou hast given me are of thee.

For I have given unto them the words which thou gavest me; and they have received them, and have known surely that I came out from thee, and they have believed that thou didst send me.

I pray for them: I pray not for the world, but for them which thou hast given me; for they are thine.

And all mine are thine, and thine are mine; and I am glorified in them.

And now I am no more in the world, but these are in the world, and I come to thee. Holy Father, keep through thine own name those whom thou hast given me, that they may be one, as we are.

While I was with them in the world, I kept them in thy name: those that thou gavest me I have kept, and none of them is lost, but the son of perdition; that the scripture might be fulfilled.

And now come I to thee; and these things I speak in the world, that they might have my joy fulfilled in themselves.

I have given them thy word; and the world hath hated them, because they are not of the world, even as I am not of the world.

I pray not that thou shouldest take them out of the world, but that thou shouldest keep them from the evil.

They are not of the world, even as I am not of the world.

Sanctify them through thy truth: thy word is truth.

As thou hast sent me into the world, even so have I also sent them into the world.

And for their sakes I sanctify myself, that they also might be sanctified through the truth.

Neither pray I for these alone, but for them also which shall believe on me through their word;

That they all may be one; as thou, Father, art in me, and I in thee, that they also may be one in us: that the world may believe that thou hast sent me.

And the glory which thou gavest me I have given them; that they may be one, even as we are one:

I in them, and thou in me, that they may be made perfect in one; and that the world may know that thou hast sent me, and hast loved them, as thou hast loved me.

Father, I will that they also, whom thou hast given me, be with me where I am; that they may behold my glory, which thou hast given me: for thou lovedst me before the foundation of the world.

O righteous Father, the world hath not known thee: but I have known thee, and these have known that thou hast sent me.

And I have declared unto them thy name, and will declare it: that the love wherewith thou hast loved me may be in them, and I in them. (John17:1-26 KJV)

Just us

A day in the park 1995

PART 9

Journals, Diaries, and Watercolours

This section is comprised of diary notes, extracts from David's journals, and one or two images of our watercolours that were particularly special to him. I thought it would be interesting for you to see a selection of David's conversations with Jesus in his own handwriting and how honestly and naturally he recorded these times. I would also like to encourage you to keep a journal, diary, or sketch pictures of dreams, of when God speaks to you and gives you visions and images. You never know how your testimony will encourage others.

10 MARCH 2012 — VISIONS FROM DAD.

① Jayne held something in her hand. She opened her hand slowly and out rolled a brilliant white light ball. This ball darted, flew, whizzed around the room. It eventually settled high in a corner shining its' light on us.

I've experienced bright lights whilst in bed. The light is so bright it comes through my eyelids — when I open my eyes briefly it's still night.

② Again in bed I saw a portal opening and brilliant white light came from it getting brighter as it opened.

10 March 2012, A ball of light

25/03/2012
I saw the cross on fire; a river
running red dropping as a
waterfall into a ravine; red
clouds in a leaden grey sky;
a chink of light from a door
in the blackness and a figure
in the doorway.
I went through the doorway
into the daylight; people were
wearing bright clothes of red
and blue; grass; blue ~~clouds~~ sky
with white summer time clouds;
and I joined with them; the
javelin was still shooting by
overhead.
                    ¡Red¬

25 March 2012

Through the doorway into the daylight

13 July 2014 approx. 5:30/6 am.
Angel is standing at bottom left of our bed. Clad in silver. Very tall, much taller than our ceiling yet not breaking through. I asked his name — Zebulon. He said

Zebulun, 19 July 2014

When we shared this event with some friends, most of them said, "What made you ask the angel's name?" David replied, "Because if I hadn't, I would never have heard the last of it from Jayne!"

Daniel 7 v10 , 12v1
Psalm 139 v 13-16 / 87v6
Exodus 32 v 32
1 Cov. 15: 41-42 / 3: 10-15
2 Cov. 5: 17 - 21

मैं हूँ
01.12.14
I am sat in an oval room faced
by a number of high polished
hardwood doors with brass fittings.
Each time I push one of these
doors the room inside is empty.
None of the rooms have anything
in them and I'm afraid to keep
trying to no avail.
I then ask Jesus to walk with me
and hold my hand. He does.
I notice a bright red painted
door with brass furniture and I
am really afraid to go through.
But Jesus holds my hand still

1 December 2014

and we enter the room. In the
room is a gold rod with a
curved top. Within this is a gold
disc. It is the heart of Jesus
and, of course the rod is His
shepherds crook
I ask Jesus to remove the heart
of stone that's within me. And
without hesitation He removes the
stone heart and implants the
gold heart (the disc from the
shepherds crook). The rod/crook
stands in the room and the gold
presence of Jesus fills the place.
Jesus takes me once more by
the hand and we walk away
from the red door room.
My rock heart has gone and a
gold heart sits in its place. in me.
My fear has gone and I walk
away with Jesus with me.
My wife Jayne was especially
a guiding factor in teasing out
my experience in this Vision.
Thankyou Lord.
                        Amen.

1 December 2014 page 2

This was an unusual vision; it was one which was
interactive for David. He could see the event taking place
as though watching a film in front of him. He was also
viewing himself in the film. He described these types of
visions as "being in time and out of time at the same time".

An angel appeared in the room, wearing a brown (unstitched) garment. I felt peaceful - he had brought peace.
A 2nd. larger angel appeared Dark-skinned, goatie beard, Etheopian looking. He wore a blue tunic - he asked if I was cold - and would I like a blanket - he had one with him. He covered me with a biscuit coloured blanket, it looked like smooth, flattened horse-hair. I felt warm and fell into a deep sleep and the angel disappeared.
• I was woken at 8:30 am for breakfast - the blanket had gone, disappeared.
About noon I was told I was being discharged and my case was being managed as an -out patient. When I left we went to see Colin to tell him what had happened.

An angel in my room, 26 February 2015

When I arrived on the hospital ward and David told me what had happened, we went to the nurses' central station together and enquired about the night-time staff. There was no one who matched the description of the angels David had seen and all of the blankets in the hospital were in their corporate colours, which was not biscuit coloured; neither did they look like smooth, flattened horse hair.

> • 27 March 2015
> I am becoming more aware
> of angels around me on a
> daily basis.
> I was walking in our back-
> garden today when I
> became aware of a figure
> dressed all in white at my side,
> not speaking, just walking.
> It then dawned on me — he
> was walking our boundary,
> with me!
> Thank you Lord.
>
> • 17 April 2015
> Dad-walk with me daily in order
> to restore my soul
> Dear Lord Jesus, I surrender
> my soul to you, and I invite
> you and welcome you to put your
> soul into me.
> David — spend ½ hour simply
> doing nothing.

27 March 2015 and 17 April 2015 angels on a daily basis

These encounters with angels took place a short while
before David was admitted for surgery on 22 April. At the
time they took place, we were not aware of what the future
held, but when we talked about them when they took place,
David said he felt a supernatural peace and felt they were
sent to help him face whatever would come next.

"Rose Cottage"

A Watercolour by David John Burgin for my
lovely wife Jayne.

I was thrilled when I saw this for the first time. It meant so much. It reminded me of the nights we spent sharing our stories with each other, and I hunted out the photograph of my great-great-grandmother standing, smiling, leaning over the garden gate and the one of great-great-grandad walking up the path with his walking stick – he does have very bow legs! We placed them by the side of the painting.

Cottages on the Beach water colour

The Northumberland coast was David's favourite place. His heart belonged to Bamburgh.

The Hope

This picture was painted from a vision David had. It was so vivid he was inspired to reproduce it as a watercolour.

Feed My Sheep

I have the original watercolour sketch of this hanging on a wall. David painted this at 11.55 p.m. one night in 2011 during a twenty-four-hour prayer vigil at a church we were visiting. The room had been set out with various artists materials for people to record what ever God showed them.

Further copies of the print of Rose Cottage can be obtained from: www.etsy.com/uk/listing/210122030/atercolour-art-print-rose-cottage-by?re=shop_home_active_1

The current range of David and Jayne's watercolours can be viewed at www.etsy.com/shop/thechocolatebantam

Till we meet again…

PART 10

+ + + + +

The Plan Revealed

Testify; tell your legacy, it is your stake in the land God has promised you and your fathers. It has more power than you think because you are His witnesses. Begin today and see what He will do if you call on His name. Your legacy in Christ is worth more than you know. His sacrifice is the only sacrifice acceptable in heaven. Heaven only recognizes Jesus's love.

David said, "God, get your glory out of this."

The thought of a gravestone with his name on it horrified David. Now I know why – he knew he would never need one. He lives. We are testifiers to life. David's love for Jesus is his legacy. The plan, all along, no matter what, is to testify to the love and power of Jesus Christ. So that all may be saved.

> At that time, Jesus answered and said, I thank thee, O Father, Lord of heaven and earth, because thou hast hid these things from the wise and prudent, and hast revealed them unto babes.

Even so, Father: for so it seemed good in thy sight.

All things are delivered unto me of my Father: and no man knoweth the Son, but the Father; neither knoweth any man the Father, save the Son, and he to whomsoever the Son will reveal him.

Come unto me, all ye that labour and are heavy laden, and I will give you rest. (Matthew 11:25-28 KJV)

Wherefore seeing we also are compassed about with so great a cloud of witnesses, let us lay aside every weight, and the sin which doth so easily beset us, and let us run with patience the race that is set before us,

Looking unto Jesus the author and finisher of our faith; who for the joy that was set before him endured the cross, despising the shame, and is set down at the right hand of the throne of God.

For consider him that endured such contradiction of sinners against himself, lest ye be wearied and faint in your minds. (Hebrews 12:1-3 KJV)

David
Jayne

The Lover:

There is nothing greater we can experience in this life than the joy of releasing the love of Jesus to people for no reward. And there is nothing more healing to the soul, nor any other thing that brings greater peace and release from all striving than to receive that love in your own heart.

My testings that have been tested are over and have become gold and silver. I am now walking in God's timing. The bloodline that was out of line is now realigned in me.

David

David lived love, but he did not demand that from me or anyone else.

> My testings that have been
> tested are over and have become
> gold and silver.
>
> I am now walking in God's timing.
> The blood-line that was out of line
> is now realigned in me.
>
> Amen.

David John Burgin
12 October 1947 – 31 December 2015
Part Two in Heaven …

The Beloved:

Only she gets to walk with him as his lover, his bride, his companion in his secret garden.

Only he has the key to unlock that which was formerly closed.

To unfasten, release and let loose that which was sealed.

Only he knows the password, the authentic word to liberate, to unchain, untie, and unfurl.

He chose her. He called her out. He unbuckled the bonds that restrained and caged her.

He ransomed her and released her from slavery and servitude.

He admitted her to his garden, gave her access to walk with him, talk with him, sit with him, as he revealed the mystery of creation and told her he loved her.

Thank you for loving me so much, my darling. I so love you. After the Song of Songs, it is our song.

> Who is this that cometh up from the wilderness, leaning upon her beloved? (Song of Solomon 8:5 KJV)

Walking with God Jesus in the perfection of His Divine balance, sharing the staggering beauty and holiness of His bride's unveiled intimacy, singing the Song of Solomon forever.

Jayne

EXTRA

My sixtieth birthday was 2 February 2017. Katie took me to the theatre in the morning, and we had a stroll around the local Thursday flea market afterwards. We mostly enjoyed identifying all the items nearly a hundred years old that were similar to or the same as those we have at home that David and I collected or have had passed down to us through our family. In the evening, Joy, Katie, and Joyce took me to a local hostelry for a birthday dinner. Joyce is our very dear friend who brought meals to our home every night when David was in hospital so that we would not have to cook or worry about preparing our own food. Joyce generously took care of our nutritional needs! During this birthday meal, a thought came into my head, and I leaned across to Joyce and said, "I need to have a few words with the Lord later about my birth certificate; I think there has been a mistake. I know it records I am sixty years old today, but I still feel twenty-one inside. Do you think the reason I don't feel 'old' is because our spirit doesn't age?"

"Of course," said Joyce without pause, and the look on her face seemed surprised I did not know that. Hmm, eureka moment. That is why when Katie saw David at the top of our stairs, he did not look as she had last seen him, but about in his thirties, without wearing spectacles and definitely younger than she had known him when Katie had first met David. Thank you, Jesus. Everything's ok.

ABOUT THE AUTHORS

A Remnant

Give ear, O my people, to my law: incline your ears to the words of my mouth.

I will open my mouth in a parable: I will utter dark sayings of old:

Which we have heard and known, and our fathers have told us.

We will not hide them from their children, shewing to the generation to come the praises of the Lord, and his strength, and his wonderful works that he has done.

For He established a testimony in Jacob, and appointed a law in Israel, which He commanded our fathers, that they should make them known to their children:

That the generation to come might know them, even the children which would be born; who should arise and declare *them* to their children:

That they may set their hope in God, and not forget the works of God, but keep his commandments. (Psalm 78:1-7 KJV)

David's Family Tree

John Shore of Barnsley, born prior 1420, made a charter in 1440 granted to William John Shore of Barnsley all his lands and tenements in Sheffield.

John Shore of Sheffield, originally of Dronfield, made his will 2 March 1682, buried at Sheffield 23 March following.

Samuel Shore Merchant of Sheffield, born 1676-1750

Samuel Shore of Sheffield afterwards of Meersbrook Esq. Born 1707-1785

John Shore of Sheffield and Norton, born 1744-1832, second surviving son of Samuel Shore of Sheffield and Meersbrook

George Shore of Sheffield and Gainsborough, born 1783-1813

George Clarke Shore, born 1807-50, married Augusta Lodge, 1 June 1843 – second wife. George was a local merchant buried at Norton Church.

Ellen Augusta Shore, born 1865-1954 (named after Ellen Lyle Shore, first wife, and Augusta Lodge, second wife).

Married William Fredrick Burgin, born 1864-1930, tram bar fitter.

Herbert Gordon Burgin, born 1895-1975, coal miner, South Yorkshire

William Henry Burgin, born 1928-79, engineer

David John Burgin, 1947-2015, architectural technician and water colourist

1) First child: Beautiful and precious unborn baby, beloved of David – together at last.

2) Second child: Beautiful and precious son, beloved of David.

3) Third child: Beautiful and precious son, beloved of David.

4) Fourth child: Beautiful and precious stepdaughter Joy, beloved of David.

5) Fifth child: Beautiful and precious stepdaughter Katie, beloved of David.

6) First grandchild: Beautiful and precious granddaughter of David.

7) Second grandchild: Beautiful and precious granddaughter of David.

The genealogy of David John Burgin has been woven into the timeless design of God's sovereignty, completing the Lord's promise to David created for His glory. It is finished.

David was born David John Burgin on 12 October 1947 in Sheffield. David worked in the construction industry as a quantity surveyor and then trained as an architectural technician. He was also a water colourist.

David became a Christian and baptized into Jesus Christ on 26 February 1984. He was baptized in the Holy Spirit and experienced many personal manifestations of the power of God. Here is a brief insight into his other loves as he described himself in his artist's biography.

"Hello, I'm David. I've been told by my wife and daughters it would be a really friendly thing to tell you a little about me and my work as an architectural illustrator and photographer. I am a Yorkshire lad. I have four grown-up children – two sons and two daughters – and two granddaughters.

"I am retired from the building industry. I have decided it is high time to indulge my private passion for drawing and painting buildings. Having been in the building industry for forty-five years I have observed, participated in, and experienced many changes in styles, construction methods, and fashions, and still conclude I love buildings, all shapes, sizes ages and styles.

"I am entranced by old castles, moody priories, derelict industrial sites that echo times of England's past. I get excited over timber-framed houses in York, the newly renovated Cruck barn in my hometown (the shutters are still up so I cannot see its face yet), the thatched cottages of Chartham Hatch (Rose Cottage is one of these), in addition, a stone-built smithy on the outskirts of Sheffield.

"I am thrilled to hear new young architects getting excited about their own projects, and when I get the opportunity, I love photographing and painting buildings with a personal appeal. From my first construction kit at the age of eight, I was hooked. When I had worked through the Book of Plans, I could design my own, with the only limitation to my imagination and experimentation, the size of the base board and somewhat limited number of component parts.

"I could easily be described as a building bore. But whether it is drawing plans, painting townscapes, city views, country cottages, or my own take on harbour life, I love losing myself in the next project and can't wait to draw out the character and beauty of the next build."

I wonder what David is doing in heaven?

Jayne was born Jayne Hubbard on 2 February 1957 in Northampton. Jayne trained as a shorthand typist and worked as a clerk in a bank in Northampton. Jayne married in 1976 and has two daughters, Joy and Katie. Jayne moved to Derbyshire in 1985.

Jayne became a Christian on 26 March 1986 and was baptized in the Holy Spirit giving glory to God. She was divorced in 1990 and came to know David in 1993. They married in a Christian Fellowship Church on 19 June 1999.

Jayne's Family Tree:

The first record of Hubbard is 1550 but script illegible.

John Hubbard married Elizabeth Marsh on 19 November 1761 at Harbeldown, Kent, England.

William Hubbard, born 1777-1862. Wood reefer and charcoal burner. Born and lived at Rose Cottage.

William Hubbard. Born 1801-? Wood reefer and charcoal burner. Born and lived at Rose Cottage.

Thomas Hubbard. Born 1828-? Wood reefer and charcoal burner. Born and lived at Rose Cottage.

John Hubbard. Born 1864-1935. Agricultural labourer. Born and lived at Rose Cottage.

Thomas Hubbard. Born 1891-1962. Dairyman stableman for dairy horses. Born and lived at Rose Cottage.

Clarence Aubrey Hubbard. Born 1917-1996. Shoemaker/ engineer.

Jayne Hubbard. Born 1957.

Joy. Born 1982.

Katie. Born 1984.

In Jesus Christ,

There Is No Such Thing As

The End

Only

Until We Meet Again ...

BIBLIOGRAPHY

King James Version (KJV)

Printed in Great Britain
by Amazon